PULP FICTION

PULP FICTION
Quentin Tarantino

THREE STORIES...
ABOUT ONE STORY...

faber and faber
LONDON · BOSTON

First published in Great Britain in 1994
by Faber and Faber Limited
3 Queen Square London WC1N 3AU

This edition is for promotional
purposes only. Not for resale.

Photoset by Parker Typesetting Service, Leicester
Printed in England by Clays Ltd, St Ives plc

This book could not have been done without the generous
co-operation of Michelle Sewell and Daryl Finer at Buena Vista
International (UK) Limited.

A CIP record for this book
is available from the British Library

ISBN 0-571-17823-5

CONTENTS

PULP FICTION was awarded the Palme d'Or at the Cannes Film Festival in May, 1994.

Among the cast were:

VINCENT VEGA	John Travolta
JULES WINNFIELD	Samuel L. Jackson
MIA WALLACE	Uma Thurman
THE WOLF	Harvey Keitel
PUMPKIN	Tim Roth
HONEY BUNNY	Amanda Plummer
FABIENNE	Maria de Medeiros
MARSELLUS WALLACE	Ving Rhames
LANCE	Eric Stolz
JODY	Rosanna Arquette
CAPTAIN KOONS	Christopher Walken
BUTCH COOLIDGE	Bruce Willis

Written and Directed by	Quentin Tarantino
Produced by	Lawrence Bender
Casting by	Ronnie Yeskel
	Gary M. Zuckerbrod
Music Supervisor	Karyn Rachtman
Costume Designer	Betsy Heimann
Production Designer	David Wasco
Editor	Sally Menke
Director of Photography	Andrzej Sekula
Co-Executive Producers	Bob Weinstein
	Harvey Weinstein
	Richard N. Gladstein
Executive Producers	Danny DeVito
	Michael Shamberg
	Stacey Sher

Stories by   Quentin Tarantino
Roger Avary

A Miramax presentation of A Band Apart and Jersey Films production.

Released in the United Kingdom by Buena Vista International (UK) Limited.

Pulp Fiction

PULP (pulp) n. 1. A soft, moist, shapeless mass of matter.

2. A magazine or book containing lurid subject matter and being characteristically printed on rough, unfinished paper

American Heritage Dictionary: New College Edition

CONTENTS

INT. COFFEE SHOP — MORNING

A normal Denny's, Spires-like coffee shop in Los Angeles. It's about 9:00 in the morning. While the place isn't jammed, there's a healthy number of people drinking coffee, munching on bacon and eating eggs.

Two of these people are a Young Man and a Young Woman. Young Man has a slight working-class English accent and, like his fellow countrymen, smokes cigarettes like they're going out of style.

It is impossible to tell where the Young Woman is from or how old she is; everything she does contradicts something she did. The boy and girl sit in a booth. Their dialogue is to be said in a rapid-pace His Girl Friday *fashion.*

> YOUNG MAN
> Forget it, it's too risky. I'm through doin' that shit.

> YOUNG WOMAN
> You always say that, the same thing every time: never again, I'm through, too dangerous.

> YOUNG MAN
> I know that's what I always say. I'm always right too.

YOUNG WOMAN

But you forget about it in a day or two.

YOUNG MAN

Yeah, well, the days of me forgettin' are over, and the days of me rememberin' have just begun.

YOUNG WOMAN

When you go on like this, you know what you sound like?

YOUNG MAN

I sound like a sensible fucking man, that's what I sound like.

YOUNG WOMAN

You sound like a duck.
(*imitates a duck*)
Quack, quack, quack, quack, quack, quack, quack . . .

YOUNG MAN

Yeah, well, take heart, 'cause you're never gonna hafta hear it again. 'Cause since I'm never gonna do it again, you're never gonna hafta hear me quack about how I'm never gonna do it again.

YOUNG WOMAN

After tonight?

The boy and girl laugh, their laughter putting a pause in there, back and forth.

YOUNG MAN
(*with a smile*)
Correct. I got all tonight to quack.

A Waitress comes by with a pot of coffee.

WAITRESS

Can I get anybody any more coffee?

YOUNG WOMAN

Oh yes, thank you.

The Waitress pours the Young Woman's coffee. The Young Man lights up another cigarette.

YOUNG MAN

I'm doin' fine.

The Waitress leaves. The Young Man takes a drag off of his smoke. The Young Woman pours a ton of cream and sugar into her coffee.

The Young Man goes right back into it.

YOUNG MAN

I mean, the way it is now, you're takin' the same fuckin' risk as when you rob a bank. You take more of a risk. Banks are easier! Federal banks ain't supposed to stop you in any way, during a robbery. They're insured, why should they give a fuck? You don't even need a gun in a federal bank. I heard about this one bloke, he walks into a federal bank with a portable phone, he gives the phone to the teller, the bloke on the other end of the phone says, 'We got this guy's little girl. If you don't give him all your money, we're gonna kill 'er.'

YOUNG WOMAN

Did it work?

YOUNG MAN

Fuckin' A it worked, that's what I'm talkin' about! Knucklehead walks into a bank with a telephone, not a pistol, not a shotgun, but a fuckin' phone, cleans the place out, and they don't even lift a fuckin' finger.

YOUNG WOMAN

Did they hurt the little girl?

YOUNG MAN

I don't know. There probably never was a little girl in the first place. W-well the point of the story isn't the little girl. The point of the story is, they robbed the bank with a telephone.

YOUNG WOMAN

Hm. You wanna rob banks?

YOUNG MAN

I'm not sayin' I wanna rob banks, I'm just illustrating if we did, it would be easier than what we been doin'.

YOUNG WOMAN

So you don't want to be a bank robber?

YOUNG MAN

Naw, all those guys are goin' down the same road, either dead or servin' twenty.

YOUNG WOMAN

And no more liquor stores?

YOUNG MAN

What have we been talking about? Yeah, no-more-liquor-stores. Besides, it ain't the giggle it usta be. Too many foreigners own liquor stores. Vietnamese, Koreans, they fuckin' don't even speak English. You tell 'em: 'Empty out the register.' They don't know what the fuck you're talkin' about. They make it too personal. We keep on, one of those gook motherfuckers's gonna make us kill 'em.

YOUNG WOMAN

I'm not gonna kill anybody.

YOUNG MAN

I don't wanna kill anybody either. But they'll probably put us in a situation where it's us or them. And if it's not the gooks, it's these old fuckin' Jews who've owned the store for fifteen fuckin' generations. You got Grandpa Irving sittin' behind the counter with a fuckin' Magnum in his hand. Try walkin' into one of those places with nothin' but a phone, see how far that gets you. Fuck it, forget it, we're out of it.

YOUNG WOMAN

Yeah, well, what then, day jobs?

YOUNG MAN
(laughing)

Not in this life.

YOUNG WOMAN

What then?

He calls to the Waitress.

YOUNG MAN

Garçon! Coffee!

Then looks to his girl.

. . . This place.

The Waitress comes by, pouring him some more.

WAITRESS
(*snotty*)

'*Garçon*' means boy.

She splits.

YOUNG WOMAN

This place? A coffee shop?

YOUNG MAN

What's wrong with that? Nobody ever robs restaurants, why not?
Bars, liquor stores, gas stations, you get your head blown off
stickin' up one of them. Restaurants, on the other hand, you catch
with their pants down. They're not expecting to get robbed. Not
as expecting, anyway.

YOUNG WOMAN
(*taking to idea*)

I bet you could cut down on the hero factor in a place like this.

YOUNG MAN

Correct. Same as banks, these places are insured. Manager, he
don't give a fuck. He's just tryin' to get ya out the door before you
start pluggin' the diners. Waitresses? Fucking forget it, no way
they takin' a bullet for the register. Busboys, some wetback gettin'
paid a dollar-fifty a hour, really gives a fuck you're stealin' from
the owner. Customers sittin' there with food in their mouths, they
don't know what's goin' on. One minute they're havin' a Denver
omelette, next minute someone's stickin' a gun in their face.

*The Young Woman visibly takes in the idea. The Young Man continues
in a low voice.*

. . . See, I got the idea last liquor store we stuck up. Remember all
the customers kept comin' in?

YOUNG WOMAN

Yeah.

YOUNG MAN

And you got the idea takin' their wallets.

YOUNG WOMAN

Uh-huh.

YOUNG MAN

Now, that was a good idea.

YOUNG WOMAN

Thank you.

YOUNG MAN

Made more from the wallets than we did the register.

YOUNG WOMAN

Yes, we did.

YOUNG MAN

A lot of people come to restaurants.

YOUNG WOMAN

A lot of wallets.

YOUNG MAN

Pretty smart, huh?

The Young Woman scans the restaurant with this new information. She sees all the patrons eating, lost in conversations. The tired Waitress, taking orders. The Busboys going through the motions, collecting dishes. The Manager complaining to the cook about something. A smile breaks out on the Young Woman's face.

YOUNG WOMAN

Pretty smart.

(*into it*)

I'm ready, let's do it, right now, right here. Come on.

YOUNG MAN

Alright, same as last time, remember? You're crowd control, I handle employees.

Mm-hm.

They kiss, then both take out their .32-caliber pistols and lay them on the table. He looks at her and she back at him.

YOUNG WOMAN
I love you, Pumpkin.

YOUNG MAN
I love you, Honey Bunny.

And with that, Pumpkin and Honey Bunny grab their weapons, stand up and rob the restaurant. Pumpkin's robbery persona is that of the in-control professional. Honey Bunny's is that of the psychopathic, hair-triggered, loose cannon.

PUMPKIN
(*yelling to all*)
Everybody be cool, this is a robbery!

HONEY BUNNY
Any of you fuckin' pricks move and I'll execute every motherfuckin' last one of you!

CUT TO:

CREDIT SEQUENCE

PULP FICTION

INT. '74 CHEVY (MOVING) – MORNING

An old gas-guzzling, dirty, white 1974 Chevy Nova barrels down a homeless-ridden street in Hollywood. In the front seat are two young fellas – one white, one black – both wearing cheap black suits with thin black ties under long green dusters. Their names are Vincent Vega (white) and Jules Winnfield (black). Jules is behind the wheel.

JULES
Okay, so, tell me about the hash bars?

VINCENT

Okay. What you want to know?

JULES

Hash is legal there, right?

VINCENT

Yeah, it's legal, but it ain't a hundred percent legal. I mean, you just can't walk into a restaurant, roll a joint, and start puffin' away. I mean, they want you to smoke in your home or certain designated places.

JULES

Those are hash bars?

VINCENT

Yeah, it breaks down like this: it's legal to buy it, it's legal to own it and, if you're the proprietor of a hash bar, it's legal to sell it. It's legal to carry it, but, but, but that doesn't matter 'cause – get a load of this, alright – if the cops stop you, it's illegal for them to search you. I mean, that's a right the cops in Amsterdam don't have.

JULES

Oh, man, I'm goin', that's all there is to it. I'm fuckin' goin'.

VINCENT

I know, baby, you'd dig it the most. But you know what the funniest thing about Europe is?

JULES

What?

VINCENT

It's the little differences. I mean, they got the same shit over there that we got here, but it's just, just, there it's a little different.

JULES

Example?

VINCENT

Well, you can walk into a movie theater and buy a beer. And I don't mean just, like, in no paper cup. I'm talking about a glass of beer. And in Paris, you can buy a beer at McDonald's. And, you know what they call a Quarter-Pounder with Cheese in Paris?

JULES

They don't call it a Quarter-Pounder with Cheese?

VINCENT

No, man, they got the metric system there, they wouldn't know what the fuck a Quarter-Pounder is.

JULES

What'd they call it?

VINCENT

They call it a Royale with Cheese.

JULES
(repeating)

Royale with Cheese.

VINCENT

Yeah, that's right.

JULES

What'd they call a Big Mac?

VINCENT

Well, Big Mac's a Big Mac, but they call it Le Big Mac.

JULES

Le Big Mac. What do they call a Whopper?

VINCENT

I dunno, I didn't go into a Burger King. But you know what they put on French fries in Holland instead of ketchup?

JULES

What?

VINCENT

Mayonnaise.

JULES

Goddamn!

VINCENT

I seen 'em do it, man. They fuckin' drown 'em in that shit.

JULES

Yuck.

CUT TO:

INT. CHEVY (TRUNK) – MORNING

The trunk of the Chevy opens up, Jules and Vincent reach inside, taking out two .45 Automatics, loading and cocking them.

JULES

We should have shotguns for this kind of deal.

VINCENT

How many up there?

JULES

Three or four.

VINCENT

Counting our guy?

JULES

I'm not sure.

VINCENT

So there could be up to five guys up there?

JULES

It's possible.

VINCENT

We should have fuckin' shotguns.

They close the trunk.

CUT TO:

EXT. APARTMENT BUILDING COURTYARD – MORNING

Vincent and Jules, their long matching overcoats practically dragging on the ground, walk through the courtyard of what looks like a hacienda-style Hollywood apartment building.

We track alongside.

What's her name?

JULES
Mia.

VINCENT
Mia. How did Marsellus and her meet?

JULES
I dunno, however people meet people. She usta be an actress.

VINCENT
Oh, really, she do anything I'd've seen?

JULES
I think her biggest deal was she starred in a pilot.

VINCENT
Pilot? What's a pilot?

JULES
Well, you know the shows on TV?

VINCENT
I don't watch TV.

JULES

Yes, but you're aware that there's an invention called television, and on this invention they show shows, right?

VINCENT

Yeah.

JULES

Well, the way they pick TV shows is, they make one show, and that show's called a 'pilot.' And then they show that one show to the people who pick the shows, and on the strength of that one show, they decide if they want to make more shows. Some get accepted and become TV programs, and some don't, and become nothing. She starred in one of the ones that became nothing.

They enter the apartment building.

INT. RECEPTION AREA (APARTMENT BUILDING) – MORNING

Vincent and Jules walk through the reception area and wait for the elevator.

JULES

You remember Antwan Rockamora? Half-black, half-Samoan, usta call him 'Tony Rocky Horror.'

VINCENT

Yeah, maybe. Fat, right?

JULES

I wouldn't go so far as to call the brother fat. He's got a weight problem. What's the nigger gonna do, he's Samoan.

VINCENT

I think I know who you mean, what about him?

JULES

Well, Marsellus fucked his ass up good. And word around the campfire is, it was on account of Marsellus Wallace's wife.

The elevator arrives, the men step inside.

18

INT. ELEVATOR – MORNING

VINCENT
So, what'd he do, fuck her?

JULES
No, no no, no, no, no, no, nothin' that bad.

VINCENT
Well, what then?

JULES
He gave her a foot massage.

VINCENT
A foot massage?

Jules nods his head: 'Yes.'

. . . That's it?

Jules nods his head: 'Yes.'

What did Marsellus do?

JULES
Sent a couple of guys over to his place. They took him out on his
patio, threw his ass over the balcony. Nigger fell four stories.
They had this garden at the bottom, enclosed in glass, like a
greenhouse – nigger fell through that. Since then, he's kinda
developed a speech impediment.

The elevator doors open, Jules and Vincent exit.

VINCENT
That's a damn shame.

INT. APARTMENT BUILDING HALLWAY – MORNING

*Steadicam in front of Jules and Vincent as they make a beeline down the
hall.*

VINCENT
Still I hafta say, play with matches, ya get burned.

JULES

Whaddya mean?

VINCENT

You don't be givin' Marsellus Wallace's new bride a foot massage.

JULES

You don't think he overreacted?

VINCENT

Well, Antwan probably didn't expect Marsellus to react like he did, but he had to expect a reaction.

JULES

It was a foot massage, a foot massage is nothing. I give my mother a foot massage.

VINCENT

No, it's laying hands on Marsellus Wallace's new wife in a familiar way. Is it as bad as eatin' her pussy out – no, but you're in the same fuckin' ballpark.

Jules stops Vincent.

JULES

Whoa . . . whoa . . . whoa . . . stop right there. Eatin' a bitch out, and givin' a bitch a foot massage, ain't even the same fuckin' thing.

VINCENT

Not the same thing, the same ballpark.

JULES

It ain't no *ballpark* either. Now look, maybe your method of massage differs from mine, but touchin' his lady's feet, and stickin' your tongue in her holiest of holies, ain't the same ballpark, ain't the same league, ain't even the same fuckin' sport. Foot massages don't mean shit.

VINCENT

Have you ever given a foot massage?

JULES

Don't be tellin' me about foot massages. I'm the fuckin' foot master.

VINCENT

Given a lot of 'em?

JULES

Shit yeah. I got my technique down man, I don't tickle or nothin'.

VINCENT

Have you ever given a guy a foot massage?

Jules looks at him a long moment – he's been set up.

JULES

Fuck you.

He starts walking down the hall. Vincent, smiling, walks a little bit behind.

VINCENT

How many?

JULES

Fuck you.

VINCENT

You know, I'm kinda tired. I could use a foot massage myself.

JULES

Yo, yo, yo. Man, you best back off, I'm gittin' pissed – this is the door.

The two men stand in front of a door numbered '49.' They whisper.

. . . What time is it?

VINCENT
(*checking his watch*)

Seven-twenty-two in the a.m.

JULES

It ain't quite time yet, let's hang back.

They move a little away from the door, facing each other, still whispering.

. . . Look just because I wouldn't give no man a foot massage, don't make it right for Marsellus to throw Antwan off a building into a glass-motherfuckin'-house, fuckin' up the way the nigger talks. That shit ain't right, man. Motherfucker do that shit to me, he better paralyze my ass, 'cause I'd kill a motherfucker, you know what I'm saying?

VINCENT

I'm not sayin' he was right, but you're sayin' a foot massage don't mean nothin', and I'm saying' it does. I've given a million ladies a million foot massages and they all meant somethin'. Now, we act like they don't, but they do. That's what's so fuckin' cool about 'em. There's a sensual thing goin' on that nobody's talkin' about, but you know it and she knows it, fuckin' Marsellus knew it, and Antwan shoulda known fuckin' better. That's his fuckin' wife, man. He ain't gonna have a sense of humor about that shit. You know what I'm saying?

JULES

That's an interesting point, but let's get into character.

VINCENT

What's her name again?

JULES

Mia. Why you so interested in big man's wife?

VINCENT

Well, Marsellus is leavin' for Florida and when he's gone, he wants me to take care of Mia.

JULES

Take care of her?

Making a gun out of his finger and placing it to his head.

VINCENT

Not that! Take her out. Show her a good time. Make sure she don't get lonely.

JULES

You're gonna be takin' Mia Wallace out on a date?

VINCENT

It ain't a date. It's like when you and your buddy's wife go to a movie or somethin'. It's just . . . you know . . . good company, that's all.

22

Jules just looks at him.

. . . It's not a date.

Jules just looks at him.

*[VINCENT
I'm not gonna be a bad boy.

Jules shakes his head and mumbles to himself.

JULES
Bitch gonna kill more niggers than time.

VINCENT
What was that?

JULES
Nothin'. Let's get into character.

VINCENT
What'd you say?

JULES
I didn't say shit. Let's go to work.

VINCENT
Don't play with me, you said somethin', now what was it?

JULES
(referring to the job)
Do you wanna do this?

VINCENT
I want you to repeat what you said.

JULES
That door's gonna open in about thirty seconds, so git yourself
together –

VINCENT
– my self is together –

* Material in brackets was cut from completed film.

JULES

– bullshit it is. Stop thinkin' 'bout that ho, and get yourself together like a qualified pro.]

INT. APARTMENT (ROOM 49) – MORNING

Three young guys, obviously in over their heads, sit at a table with hamburgers, French fries and soda pops laid out.

One of them flips the loud bolt on the door, opening it to reveal Jules and Vincent in the hallway.

JULES

Hey kids.

The two men stroll inside.

The three young caught-off-guard Guys are:

Marvin

The black young man, who opened the door, will, as the scene progresses, back into the corner.

Roger

A young blond-haired surfer kid with a 'flock of seagulls' haircut.

Brett

A white, preppy-looking sort with a blow-dry haircut sits at the table with a big sloppy hambuger in his hand.

Vincent and Jules take in the place, with their hands in their pockets. Jules is the one who does the talking.

JULES

How you boys doin'?

No answer.

(to Brett)
. . . Am I trippin', or did I just ask you a question?

BRETT

We're doin' okay.

As Jules and Brett talk, Vincent moves behind the young Guys.

JULES

Do you know who we are?

Brett shakes his head: 'No.'

. . . We're associates of your business partner Marsellus Wallace. You do remember your business partner, don't ya?

No answer.

JULES
(*to Brett*)

Now, I'm gonna take a wild guess here: you're Brett, right?

BRETT

Yeah.

JULES

I thought so. Well, you remember your business partner Marsellus Wallace, don't ya Brett?

BRETT

I remember him.

JULES

Good for you. Looks like me and Vincent caught you boys at breakfast. Sorry 'bout that. What'cha eatin'?

BRETT

Hamburgers.

JULES

Hamburgers. The cornerstone of any nutritious breakfast. What kinda hamburgers?

BRETT

Cheeseburgers.

JULES

No, no no, no no. I mean where did you get 'em? McDonald's, Wendy's, Jack-in-the-Box, where?

BRETT

Big Kahuna Burger.

JULES

Big Kahuna Burger. That's that Hawaiian burger joint. I heard
they got some tasty burgers. I ain't never had one myself, how are
they?

BRETT

They're good.

JULES

You mind if I try one of yours?

BRETT

No.

JULES

Yours is this one, right?

BRETT

Yeah.

Jules grabs the burger and takes a bite of it.

JULES

Uuummmm, that's a tasty burger.

(*to Vincent*)

Vincent, you ever had a Big Kahuna Burger?

VINCENT

No.

Jules holds out the Big Kahuna.

JULES

You wanna bite, they're real good.

VINCENT

I ain't hungry.

JULES

Well, if you like hamburgers give 'em a try sometime. Me, I can't
usually eat 'em 'cause my girlfriend's a vegetarian. Which more or
less makes me a vegetarian, but I sure love the taste of a good burger.

26

(*to Brett*)

You know what they call a Quarter-Pounder with Cheese in France?

BRETT

No.

JULES

Tell 'em, Vincent.

VINCENT

Royale with Cheese.

JULES

Royale with Cheese. You know why they call it that?

BRETT

Because of the metric system?

JULES

Check out the big brain on Brett. You'a smart motherfucker, that's right. The metric system.

(*he points at a fast food drink cup*)

What's in this?

BRETT

Sprite.

JULES

Sprite, good. You mind if I have some of your tasty beverage to wash this down with?

BRETT

Sure.

Jules grabs the cup and takes a sip.

JULES

Uuuuummmm, hits the spot!

(*to Roger*)

You, Flock of Seagulls, you know what we're here for?

Roger nods his head: 'Yes.'

Then why don't you tell my man Vince here where you got the shit hid.

MARVIN

It's over there –

JULES

– I don't remember askin' you a goddamn thing.
(*to Roger*)
You were sayin'?

ROGER

It's in the cupboard.

Vincent looks in a cupboard, bends down, then comes up holding a black snap briefcase.

VINCENT

Got it.

Vincent flips the two locks, opening the case. We can't see what's inside, but a small glow emits from the case. Vincent just stares at it, transfixed.

JULES

We happy?

No answer from the transfixed Vincent.

. . . Vincent!

Vincent looks up at Jules.

. . . We happy?

Closing the case.

VINCENT

We're happy.

BRETT
(*to Jules*)
Look, what's your name? I got his name's Vincent, but what's yours?

JULES

My name's Pitt, and you ain't talkin' your ass outta this shit.

BRETT

I just want you to know how sorry we are about how fucked up things got between us and Mr Wallace. When we entered into this thing, we only had the best intentions –

As Brett talks, Jules takes out his gun and shoots Roger three times in the chest, blowing him out of his chair.

Vince smiles to himself. Jules has got style.

Brett has just shit his pants. He's not crying or whimpering, but he's so full of fear, it's as if his body is imploding.

JULES
(*to Brett*)

Oh, I'm sorry. Did that break your concentration? I didn't mean to do that. Please continue. I believe you were saying something about 'best intentions.'

Brett can't say a word.

Whatsamatter? Oh, you were through anyway. Well, allow me to retort. Would you describe for me what Marsellus Wallace looks like?

Brett still can't speak.

Jules snaps, savagely tipping the card table over, removing the only barrier between himself and Brett. Brett now sits in a lone chair before Jules like a political prisoner in front of an interrogator.

JULES

What country you from!

BRETT
(*petrified*)

What?

JULES

'What' ain't no country I know! Do they speak English in 'What?'

BRETT
(*near heart attack*)

What?

JULES

English-motherfucker-can-you-speak-it?

BRETT

Yes.

JULES

Then you understand what I'm sayin'?

BRETT

Yes.

JULES

Now describe what Marsellus Wallace looks like!

BRETT
(*out of fear*)

What?

Jules takes his .45 and presses the barrel hard in Brett's cheek.

JULES

Say 'What' again! C'mon, say 'What' again! I dare ya, I double dare ya, motherfucker. Say 'What' one more goddamn time!

Brett is regressing on the spot.

. . . Now describe to me what Marsellus Wallace looks like!

Brett does his best.

BRETT

Well he's . . . he's . . . black –

JULES

– go on!

BRETT

. . . and he's . . . he's . . . bald –

JULES

– does he look like a bitch?!

BRETT
(*without thinking*)

What?

Jules' eyes go to Vincent, Vincent smirks, Jules rolls his eyes and shoots Brett in the shoulder.

Brett screams, breaking into a shaking/trembling spasm in the chair.

JULES

Does-he-look-like-a-bitch?!

BRETT
(*in agony*)

No.

JULES

Then why did you try to fuck 'im like a bitch?!

BRETT
(*in spasm*)

I didn't.

Now in a lower voice.

JULES

Yes ya did, Brett. Ya tried ta fuck 'im and Marsellus Wallace don't like to be fucked by anybody except Missus Wallace. You ever read the Bible, Brett?

BRETT
(*in spasm*)

Yes.

JULES

There's a passage I got memorized, seems appropriate for this situation: Ezekiel 25:17. 'The path of the righteous man is beset on all sides by the inequities of the selfish and the tyranny of evil men. Blessed is he who, in the name of charity and good will, shepherds the weak through the valley of darkness, for he is truly his brother's keeper and the finder of lost children. And I will strike down upon thee with great vengeance and furious anger those who attempt to poison and destroy my brothers. And you will know my name is the Lord when I lay my vengeance upon you.'

The two men empty their guns at the same time on the sitting Brett. Marvin collapses into a heap in the corner.

*[When they are finished, the bullet-ridden carcass just sits there for a moment, then topples over.

All is quiet.

The only sound is Marvin muttering in the corner.

> MARVIN
> . . . goddamn . . . goddamn . . . that was fucked up . . . goddamn, that was cold-blooded . . .

> VINCENT
> (*pointing to Marvin*)
> Friend of yours?

> JULES
> Yeah, Marvin-Vincent-Vincent-Marvin.

> VINCENT
> Tell 'im to shut up, he's gettin' on my nerves.

> JULES
> Marvin, I'd knock that shit off if I was you.

Then suddenly the bathroom door bursts open, and a Fourth Man (as young as the rest) comes charging out, a silver Magnum in his hand.

> FOURTH MAN
> Die . . . die . . . die . . . die . . . die . . . die!

The Fourth Man fires six booming shots from his hand cannon in the direction of Vincent and Jules. He screams a maniacal cry of revenge until he's dry firing.

Then . . . his face does a complete change of expression. It goes from a 'Vengeance is mine' expression, to a 'What the fuck' blank look.

> FOURTH MAN
> I don't understand –

---

* Cut from completed film.

The Fourth Man is blown off his feet and out of frame by bullets that tear him to shreds.

He leaves the frame empty.

   FADE TO BLACK]

AGAINST BLACK, TITLE CARD:

'VINCENT VEGA
AND
MARSELLUS WALLACE'S WIFE'

FADE IN:

MEDIUM SHOT — BUTCH COOLIDGE

We fade up on Butch Coolidge, a white, 26-year-old prizefighter. Butch sits at a table wearing a red and blue high-school athletic jacket. Talking to him off screen is everybody's boss Marsellus Wallace. The black man sounds like a cross between a gangster and a king.

MARSELLUS
(*off*)

I think you're gonna find – when all this shit is over and done – I think you're gonna find yourself one smilin' motherfucker. Thing is, Butch, right now you got ability. But painful as it may be, ability don't last. And your days are just about over. Now that's a hard motherfuckin' fact of life, but it's a fact of life your ass is gonna hafta git realistic about. This business is filled to the brim with unrealistic motherfuckers who thought their ass would age like wine. Besides, even if you went all the way, what would you be? Featherweight champion of the world. Who gives a shit? I doubt you can even get a credit card based on that.

A hand lays an envelope full of money on the table in front of Butch. Butch picks it up.

. . . Now the night of the fight, you may feel a slight sting. That's pride fuckin' wit ya. Fuck pride! Pride only hurts, it never helps.

Fight through that shit. 'Cause a year from now, when you're
kickin' it in the Caribbean you're gonna say, 'Marsellus Wallace
was right.'

> BUTCH

I got no problems with that, Mr Wallace.

> MARSELLUS
> (*off*)

In the fifth, your ass goes down.

Butch nods his head: 'Yes.'

Say it!

> BUTCH

In the fifth, my ass goes down.

CUT TO:

INT. CAR (MOVING) – DAY

*Vincent Vega looks really cool behind the wheel of a 1964 cherry-red
Chevy Malibu convertible. From the car radio, rockabilly music plays.
The background is a colorful process shot.*

EXT. SALLY LEROY'S – DAY

Sally LeRoy's is a large topless bar by LAX that Marsellus owns.

*Vincent's classic Malibu whips into the near empty parking lot and parks
next to a white Honda Civic.*

*Vince knocks on the door. The front entrance is unlocked, revealing the
Dapper Dan fellow on the inside: English Dave. Dave isn't really
English, he's a young black man from Baldwin Park, who has run a few
clubs for Marsellus, including Sally LeRoy's.*

> ENGLISH DAVE

Vincent Vega, our man in Amsterdam. Jules Winnfield our man
in Inglewood. Git your asses on in here.

Vincent and Jules, wearing shorts and T-shirts, step inside.

Goddamn, nigger, what's up with them clothes?

> JULES

You don't even want to know.

English Dave slams the door in our faces.

INT. SALLY LEROY'S — DAY

The spacious club is empty this time of day. English Dave crosses to the bar, and Vince follows.

> VINCENT

Where's big man?

> ENGLISH DAVE

He's over there, finishing up some business.

VINCENT'S POV

Butch shakes hands with a huge figure with his back to us. The huge figure is the infamous and as yet still unseen Marsellus.

> ENGLISH DAVE
> (off)

Hang back for a second or two, and when you see the white boy leave, go on over. In the meanwhile, can I make you an espresso?

> VINCENT

How 'bout a cup of just plain ol' American?

> ENGLISH DAVE

Comin' up. I hear you're taking Mia out tomorrow?

> VINCENT

At Marsellus' request.

> ENGLISH DAVE

Have you met Mia?

> VINCENT

Not yet.

English Dave smiles to himself. Jules chuckles.

What's so funny?

ENGLISH DAVE

Not a goddamn thing.

JULES

I gotta piss.

VINCENT

Look, I'm not an idiot. She's the big man's fuckin' wife. I'm
gonna sit across a table, chew my food with my mouth closed,
laugh at her jokes and that's all I'm gonna do.

English Dave puts Vince's coffee in front of him.

ENGLISH DAVE

Hey, my name's Paul, and this is between y'all.

VINCENT

Then what'd you fuckin' ask me about it for? Asshole.

Butch bellies up to the bar next to Vincent.

BUTCH
(*to English Dave*)

Can I get a pack'a Red Apples?

ENGLISH DAVE

Filters?

BUTCH

Non.

*While Butch waits for his smokes, Vincent just sips his coffee, staring at
him. Butch looks over at him.*

Lookin' at somethin', friend?

VINCENT

I ain't your friend, palooka.

Butch does a slow burn toward Vincent.

BUTCH

What was that?

37

VINCENT

I think ya heard me just fine, punchy.

Butch turns his body to Vincent, when . . .

MARSELLUS
(*off*)

Vincent Vega has entered the building, git your ass over here!

Vincent walks forward out of frame, never giving Butch another glance. We dolly into CU *on Butch, left alone in the frame, looking like he's ready to go into the manners-teaching business.*

BUTCH'S POV

Vincent hugging and kissing the obscured figure that is Marsellus.

Butch makes the wise decision that if this asshole's a friend of Marsellus, he better let it go – for now.

ENGLISH DAVE
(*off*)

Pack of Red Apples, dollar-forty.

Butch is snapped out of his ass-kicking thoughts. He pays English Dave and walks out of the shot.

DISSOLVE TO:

INT. LANCE'S HOUSE (KITCHEN) – NIGHT

CU JODY

A woman who appears to have a fondness for earrings. Both of her ears are pierced five times. She also sports rings in her lip, eyebrows and nose.

JODY

. . . I'll lend it to you. It's a great book on body-piercing.

Jody, Vincent and a young woman named Trudi sit at the kitchen table of a suburban house in Echo Park. Even though Vince is at the same table, he's not included in the conversation.

TRUDI

You know how they use that gun when they pierce your ears?

They don't use that when they pierce your nipples, do they?

JODY

Forget that gun. That gun goes against the entire idea behind piercing. All of my piercing, sixteen places on my body, every one of 'em done with a needle. Five in each ear. One through the nipple of my left breast. One through my right nostril. One through my left eyebrow. One through my lip. One in my clit. And I wear a stud in my tongue.

Vince has been letting this conversation go through one ear and out the other, until that last remark.

VINCENT
(*interrupting*)

Excuse me, sorry to interrupt. I'm curious, why would you get a stud in your tongue?

Jody looks at him and says as if it were the most obvious thing in the world.

JODY

It's a sex thing. It helps fellatio.

That thought never occurred to Vincent, but he can't deny it makes sense. Jody continues talking to Trudi, leaving Vincent to ponder the truth of her statement.

> LANCE
> (*off*)
Vincenzo, step into my office.

INT. LANCE'S BEDROOM – NIGHT

Lance, late-twenties, is a young man with a wild and woolly appearance that goes hand-in-hand with his wild and woolly personality. Lance has been selling drugs his entire adult life. He's never had a day job, never filed a tax return and has never been arrested. He wears a red flannel shirt over a 'Speed Racer' T-shirt.

Three bags of heroin lie on Lance's bed.

Lance and Vincent stand at the foot of the bed.

> LANCE
Now this is Panda, from Mexico. Very good stuff. This is Bava, different, but equally good. And this is Choco from the Harz Mountains of Germany. Now the first two are the same, forty-five an ounce – those are friend prices – but this one . . .
> (*pointing to the Choco*)
. . . this one's a little more expensive. It's fifty-five. But when you shoot it, you'll know where that extra money went. Nothing wrong with the first two. It's real, real, real, good shit. But this one's a fuckin' madman.

> VINCENT
Remember, I just got back from Amsterdam.

> LANCE
Am I a nigger? Are you in Inglewood? No. You're in my home. White people who know the difference between good shit and bad shit, this is the house they come to. My shit, I'll take the Pepsi challenge with Amsterdam shit any ol' day of the fuckin' week.

> VINCENT
That's a bold statement.

LANCE

This ain't Amsterdam, Vince. This is a seller's market. Coke is
fuckin' dead as disco. Heroin's comin' back in a big fuckin' way.
It's this whole seventies retro. Bell bottoms, heroin, they're as hot
as hell.

Vincent takes out a roll of money that would choke a horse to death.

VINCENT

Give me three hundred worth of the madman. If it's as good as
you say, I'll be back for a thousand.

LANCE

I just hope I still have it. I'm givin' ya some out of my own private
stash. That's what a nice guy I am.

Lance pulls out some items from a wooden box.

. . . Hey, I'm outta balloons. Is a baggie alright?

VINCENT

Yeah. That's cool.

Lance opens door toward kitchen.

LANCE

Alright. I'll just get it for ya.

(*to Jody*)

Honey, will you get me some baggies and twistix from the
kitchen?

JODY
(*off*)

Okay.

Lance shuts the door.

LANCE

Whaddya think of Trudi? She ain't got a boyfriend, wanna hang
out an' get high?

VINCENT

Which one's Trudi? The one with all the shit in her face?

LANCE

No, that's Jody. That's my wife.

Vincent and Lance giggle at the 'faux pas.'

VINCENT

I'm on my way somewhere. I got a dinner engagement. Rain check?

LANCE

No problemo.

Jody enters and gives Lance the baggies and twistix. Lance divides the heroin while Vincent takes out his case of works (utensils for shooting up).

VINCENT

You don't mind if I shoot up here?

LANCE

Me casa, su casa.

VINCENT

Mucho gracias.

Vincent takes his works out of his case and, as the two continue to talk, Vince shoots up.

LANCE

Still got your Malibu?

VINCENT

You know what some fucker did to it the other day?

LANCE

What?

VINCENT

Fuckin' keyed it.

LANCE

Oh man, that's fucked up.

VINCENT

Tell me about it. I had the goddamn thing in storage three years. It's out five fuckin' days – five days, and some dickless piece of shit fucks with it.

LANCE

They should be fuckin' killed. No trial, no jury, straight to execution.

As he cooks his heroin –

> VINCENT
>
> I just wish I caught 'em doin' it, ya know? Oh man, I'd give anything to catch 'em doin' it. It'a been worth him doin' it, if I coulda just caught 'em, you know what I mean?

> LANCE
>
> What a fucker!

> VINCENT
>
> It's chicken shit. You don't fuck another man's vehicle.

> LANCE
>
> YOU DON'T DO IT.

> VINCENT
>
> It's just against the rules.

CU – THE NEEDLE
going into Vincent's vein.

CU – BLOOD
spurting back into the syringe, mixing with the heroin.

CU OF VINCENT'S THUMB
pushing down on the plunger.

CUT TO:

*[EXT. MARSELLUS WALLACE'S HOUSE – NIGHT

Vincent walks up to the driveway leading to Marsellus Wallace's front door. When he gets to the door, he hears music on the other side, and a note in plain view taped to it. He rips it off.

CU – NOTE

> *Hi Vincent,*
> *I'm getting dressed. The door's*
> *open. Come inside and make*
> *yourself a drink.*
>> *Mia*

* Cut from completed film.

Vincent neatly folds the note up, sticks it in his pocket, takes a here-goes-nothing breath and turns the knob.

INT. MARSELLUS WALLACE'S HOUSE – NIGHT

As Vincent steps inside, the music that was behind the door swells drastically. Vincent, hands in pockets, strolls inside, checking out his boss's home.

> VINCENT
> (yelling)

Hello! I'm here!

We hear a door open, Vincent turns in its direction.

INT. DRESSING ROOM – NIGHT

We're inside the room where the music is playing. In the foreground Mia Wallace, naked with her back to us, talks to Vincent through a crack in the door. The door shields the front of her body from Vincent.

> MIA

Vincent Vega?

> VINCENT

I'm Vincent, you Mia?

> MIA

That's me, pleased to meetcha. I'm still getting dressed. To your left, past the kitchen, is a bar. Why don't you make yourself a drink, have a seat in the living room, and I'll be out within three shakes of a lamb's tail.

> VINCENT

Take your time.

Mia closes the door. Before she can fully turn around and show us her face . . .

WE CUT:

BACK TO VINCENT
standing where he was, music beating, looking at the closed door. We slowly zoom to the door.

We slowly zoom from a medium shot to CU *on Vincent as he contemplates what's on the other side of the door. When we reach a* CU*, he walks out of frame, breaking the spell.*

Vincent walks to the bar and pours himself a drink.

WE JUXTAPOSE
as the music plays.

Mia's dress selection is taken out of the closet.

Vincent, drink in hand, moves into the living room.

Mia, her back to camera, dressed in her pretty dress, checks herself in the mirror. We dolly towards her. Her face is still obscured.

CU – PORTRAIT OF MIA
hanging on the living-room wall, showing Mia sensually reclining on a couch.

HIGH ANGLE SHOT OF VINCENT
looking up at the portrait.

CU – *Mia cutting a huge line of coke on her vanity table with a credit card.*

Vincent sits on a plush, comfy couch.

CU – MIA'S NOSE
snorting the line from a rolled up dollar bill.

Vincent on the couch, drink in hand. The song abruptly cuts off.

CU – CD PLAYER OPENING
Mia's hand comes in and takes the CD out.

The camera follows behind Mia's bare feet as she walks out of the dressing room, through the dining room, through the kitchen and into the living room.

SHOT THROUGH A VIDEO CAMERA
Mia has a camcorder and is videotaping Vincent on the couch. He looks up and sees her.

> MIA
> (*off*)
> Smile, you're on Mia's camera!

VINCENT

Ready to go?

MIA
(*off*)

Not yet, I'm going to interview you first. Are you any relation to Suzanne Vega?

VINCENT

Yeah, she's my cousin.

MIA
(*off*)

Suzanne Vega the folk singer is your cousin?

VINCENT

Suzanne Vega's my cousin. If she's become a folk singer, I sure as hell don't know nothin' about it. But then I haven't been to too many Thanksgivings lately.

MIA
(*off*)

Now I'm gonna ask you a bunch of quick questions I've come up with that more or less tell me what kind of person I'm having dinner with. My theory is that when it comes to important subjects, there's only two ways a person can answer. For instance, there's two kinds of people in this world, Elvis people and Beatles people. Now Beatles people can like Elvis. And Elvis people can like the Beatles. But nobody likes them both equally. Somewhere you have to make a choice. And that choice tells me who you are.

VINCENT

I can dig it.

MIA
(*off*)

I knew you could. First question, Brady Bunch or The Partridge Family?

VINCENT

The Partridge Family all the way, no comparison.

MIA
(*off*)

On 'Rich Man, Poor Man,' who did you like, Peter Strauss or
Nick Nolte?

VINCENT

Nick Nolte, of course.

MIA

Are you a 'Bewitched' man, or a 'Jeannie' man?

VINCENT

'Bewitched,' all the way, though I always dug how Jeannie always
called Larry Hagman 'master.'

MIA
(*off*)

If you were Archie, who would you fuck first, Betty or Veronica?

VINCENT

Betty. I never understood Veronica's attraction.

MIA
(*off*)

Have you ever fantasized about being beaten up by a girl?

VINCENT

Sure.

MIA
(*off*)

Who?

VINCENT

Emma Peel on 'The Avengers.' That tough girl who usta hang out
with Encyclopedia Brown. And Arlene Motika.

MIA
(*off*)

Who's Arlene Motika?

VINCENT

Girl from sixth grade, you don't know her.

CU – MIA
lowers the camcorder from in front of her face and we get our first full-on

47

look at her. When we do, we get a pretty good idea why Marsellus feels the way he does. She breaks out in a blinding smile.

                              MIA
   Cut. Print. Let's go eat.]

*[[EXT. MARCELLUS WALLACE'S HOUSE — NIGHT

Vincent walks toward the house and pulls a note off the door.

CU — NOTE
The note reads:

   Hi Vincent,
   I'm getting dressed. The door's
   open. Come inside and make
   yourself a drink.
                    Mia

                              MIA
                          (*voiceover*)
   Hi, Vincent. I'm getting dressed. The door's open. Come inside
   and make yourself a drink. Mia.

FADE TO WHITE
                          (*music in*)

FADE TO:

INT. MARCELLUS' HOUSE/LIVING ROOM — NIGHT

Vincent enters in the background.

                           VINCENT
   Hello?

INT. MARSELLUS' HOUSE/DRESSING ROOM — NIGHT

*Mia, Marsellus' beautiful young wife. Video screens are in the
background. Dusty Springfield is singing 'Son of a Preacher Man.' Mia's
mouth comes toward a microphone.*

* Added during filming.

                              48

                              MIA
                        (*into microphone*)
Vincent.

INT. MARSELLUS' HOUSE/LIVING ROOM – NIGHT

Vincent turns.

                              MIA
                        (*over intercom*)
Vincent. I'm on the intercom.

                            VINCENT
Where is, where is the intercom?

INT. MARSELLUS' HOUSE/DRESSING ROOM – NIGHT

                              MIA
                        (*into microphone*)
It's on the wall by the two African fellas.

INT. MARSELLUS' HOUSE/LIVING ROOM – NIGHT

                              MIA
                        (*over intercom*)
To your right.

Vincent walks.

. . . Warm. Warmer. Disco.

Vincent finds the intercom on the wall.

                            VINCENT
Hello.

                              MIA
                        (*over intercom*)
Push the button if you want to talk.

                            VINCENT
                        (*into intercom*)
Hello.

INT. MARSELLUS' HOUSE/DRESSING ROOM – NIGHT

> MIA
> (*into microphone*)
>
> Go make yourself a drink, and I'll be down in two shakes of a lamb's tail.

INT. MARSELLUS' HOUSE/LIVING ROOM – NIGHT

> MIA
> (*over intercom*)
>
> The bar's by the fireplace.

> VINCENT
> (*into intercom*)
>
> Okay.
>
> (*licks lips*)

INT. MARSELLUS' HOUSE/DRESSING ROOM – NIGHT

A video screen with an image of Vincent, walking. The Dusty Springfield song continues.

Mia turns a knob which controls the movement of the video camera in Marcellus' living room.

INT. MARSELLUS' HOUSE/LIVING ROOM – NIGHT

Vincent picks up a bottle of scotch. He sniffs the bottle, and then pours it into a glass.

INT. MARSELLUS' HOUSE/DRESSING ROOM – NIGHT

A razor blade cuts cocaine on a mirror.

INT. MARSELLUS' HOUSE/LIVING ROOM – NIGHT

Vincent drinks a glass of scotch.

INT. MARSELLUS' HOUSE/DRESSING ROOM – NIGHT

Mia sniffs the cocaine.

INT. MARSELLUS' HOUSE/LIVING ROOM – NIGHT

Vincent sips his drink and looks at a portrait of Mia on the wall.

Mia walks into the room, and takes the needle off a record. The Dusty Springfield song stops.

> MIA
>
> Let's go.]]

EXT. JACKRABBIT SLIM'S – NIGHT

In the past six years, 1950s diners have sprung up all over LA, giving Thai restaurants a run for their money. They're all basically the same. Decor out of an 'Archie' comic book, golden oldies constantly emanating from a bubbly Wurlitzer, saucy waitresses in bobby socks, menus with items like the Fats Domino Cheeseburger, or the Wolfman Jack Omelette, and over-prices that pay for all this bullshit.

But then there's Jackrabbit Slim's, the big mama of 1950s diners. Either the best or the worst, depending on your point of view.

Vincent's Malibu pulls up to the restaurant. A big sign with a neon figure of a cartoon surly cool-cat jackrabbit in a red windbreaker towers over the establishment. Underneath the cartoon is the name: Jackrabbit Slim's. Underneath that is the slogan: 'Next best thing to a time machine.'

> *[[VINCENT
>
> What the fuck is this place?

> MIA
>
> This is Jackrabbit Slim's. An Elvis man should love it.

> VINCENT
>
> Come on, Mia, let's go get a steak.

* Added during filming.

MIA

You can get a steak here, daddy-o. Don't be a . . .

Mia draws a square with her hands. Dotted lines appear on the screen, forming a square. The lines disperse.

VINCENT

After you, kitty-cat.]]

INT. JACKRABBIT SLIM'S – NIGHT

Compared to the interior, the exterior was that of a quaint English pub. Posters from 1950s A.I.P. movies are all over the wall ('ROCK ALL NIGHT,' 'HIGH SCHOOL CONFIDENTIAL,' 'ATTACK OF THE CRAB MONSTER' and 'MACHINE GUN KELLY'). The booths that the patrons sit in are made out of the cut up bodies of 1950s cars.

In the middle of the restaurant is a dance floor. A big sign on the wall states, 'No shoes allowed.' So wannabe beboppers (actually Melrose-types) do the twist in their socks or barefeet.

The picture windows don't look out on the street, but instead, B & W movies of 1950s street scenes play behind them. The waitresses and waiters are made up as replicas of 1950s icons: Marilyn Monroe, Zorro, James Dean, Donna Reed, Martin and Lewis, and The Philip Morris Midget, wait on tables wearing appropriate costumes.

Vincent and Mia study the menu in a booth made out of a red 1959 Edsel. Buddy Holly (their waiter) comes over, sporting a big button on his chest that says: 'Hi I'm Buddy, pleasing you pleases me.'

BUDDY

Hi I'm Buddy, what can I get'cha?

VINCENT

I'll have the Douglas Sirk steak.

BUDDY

How d'ya want it, burnt to a crisp, or bloody as hell?

VINCENT

Bloody as hell. And to drink, a vanilla coke.

BUDDY

How 'bout you, Peggy Sue?

MIA

I'll have the Durwood Kirby burger – bloody – and a five-dollar
shake.

BUDDY

How d'ya want that shake, Martin and Lewis, or Amos and Andy?

MIA

Martin and Lewis.

VINCENT

Did you just order a five-dollar shake?

MIA

Sure did.

VINCENT

A shake? Milk and ice cream?

MIA

Uh-huh.

VINCENT

It cost five dollars?

BUDDY

Yep.

VINCENT

You don't put bourbon in it or anything?

BUDDY

Nope.

VINCENT

Just checking.

Buddy exits.

*Vincent takes a look around the place. The Yuppies are dancing, the Diners
are biting into big, juicy hamburgers, and the icons are playing their parts.
Marilyn is squealing, The Midget is paging Philip Morris, Donna Reed is
making her customers drink their milk, and Dean and Jerry are acting the fool.*

                              MIA
Whaddya think?

                           VINCENT
It's like a wax museum with a pulse rate.

Vincent takes out his pouch of tobacco and begins rolling himself a smoke.

After a second of watching him –

                              MIA
What are you doing?

                           VINCENT
Rollin' a smoke.

                              MIA
Here?

                           VINCENT
It's just tobacco.

                              MIA
Oh. Well in that case, will you roll me one, cowboy?

As he finishes licking it –

                           VINCENT
You can have this one, cowgirl.

He hands her the rolled smoke. She takes it, putting it to her lips. Out of nowhere appears a Zippo lighter in Vincent's hand. He lights it.

                              MIA
Thanks.

                           VINCENT
Think nothing of it.

He begins rolling one for himself.

At this time, the sound of a subway car fills the diner, making everything shake and rattle. Marilyn Monroe runs to a square vent in the floor. An imaginary subway train blows the skirt of her white dress around her ears as she lets out a squeal. The entire restaurant applauds.

Back to Mia and Vincent.

MIA

Marsellus said you just got back from Amsterdam.

VINCENT

Sure did. I heard you did a pilot.

MIA

That was my fifteen minutes.

VINCENT

What was it?

MIA

It was a show about a team of female secret agents called 'Fox Force
Five.'

VINCENT

What?

MIA

'Fox Force Five.' Fox, as in we're a bunch of foxy chicks. Force, as
in we're a force to be reckoned with. Five, as in there's one . . . two
. . . three . . . four . . . five of us. There was a blonde one,
Sommerset O'Neal from that show 'Baton Rouge,' she was the
leader. A Japanese one, a black one, a French one and a brunette
one, me. We all had special skills. Sommerset had a photographic
memory, the Japanese fox was a kung fu master, the black girl was a
demolition expert, the French fox's specialty was sex . . .

VINCENT

What was your specialty?

MIA

Knives. The character I played, Raven McCoy, her background
was she was raised by circus performers. So she grew up doing a
knife act. According to the show, she was the deadliest woman in
the world with a knife. But because she grew up in a circus, she was
also something of an acrobat. She could do illusions, she was a
trapeze artist – when you're keeping the world safe from evil, you
never know when being a trapeze artist's gonna come in handy.
And she knew a zillion old jokes her grandfather, an old
vaudevillian, taught her. If we woulda got picked up, they woulda
worked in a gimmick where every episode I woulda told an old joke.

VINCENT

Do you remember any of the jokes?

MIA

Well I only got the chance to say one, 'cause we only did one show.

VINCENT

Tell me.

MIA

No. It's really corny.

VINCENT

C'mon, don't be that way. Tell me.

MIA

No. You won't like it and I'll be embarrassed.

VINCENT

You told it in front of fifty million people and you can't tell it to me? I promise I won't laugh.

MIA
(*laughing*)

That's what I'm afraid of.

VINCENT

That's not what I meant and you know it.

MIA

You're quite the silver tongue devil, aren't you?

VINCENT

I meant I wouldn't laugh at you.

MIA

That's not what you said, Vince. Well, now I'm definitely not gonna tell ya, 'cause it's been built up too much.

VINCENT

What a gyp.

Buddy comes back with the drinks. Mia wraps her lips around the straw of her shake.

MIA

Yummy!

VINCENT

Can I have a sip of that? I'd like to know what a five-dollar shake tastes like.

MIA

Be my guest.

She slides the shake over to him.

You can use my straw, I don't have kooties.

Vincent smiles.

VINCENT

Yeah, but maybe I do.

MIA

Kooties I can handle.

He takes a sip.

VINCENT

Goddamn! That's a pretty fuckin' good milkshake.

MIA

Told ya.

VINCENT

I don't know if it's worth five dollars, but it's pretty fuckin' good.

He slides the shake back.

Then the first uncomfortable silence happens.

MIA

Don't you hate that?

VINCENT

What?

MIA

Uncomfortable silences. Why do we feel it's necessary to talk about bullshit in order to be comfortable?

VINCENT

I don't know. That's a good question.

MIA

That's when you know you found somebody special. When you can just shut the fuck up for a minute, and comfortably share silence.

VINCENT

Well, I don't think we're there yet. But don't feel bad, we just met each other.

MIA

I'll tell you what, I'll go to the bathroom and powder my nose while you sit here and think of something to say.

VINCENT

I'll do that.

INT. JACKRABBIT SLIM'S (LADIES ROOM) — NIGHT

Mia powders her nose by doing a big line of coke off the bathroom sink. Her head jerks up from the rush.

MIA
(*imitating Steppenwolf*)

I said goddamn!

INT. JACKRABBIT SLIM'S (DINING AREA) — NIGHT

Vincent digs into his Douglas Sirk steak. As he chews, his eyes scan the Hellsapopinish restaurant.

Mia comes back to the table.

MIA

Don't you love it when you go to the bathroom and you come back to find your food waiting for you?

VINCENT

We're lucky we got it at all. Buddy Holly doesn't seem to be much of a waiter. We shoulda sat in Marilyn Monroe's section.

Which one, there's two Marilyn Monroes.

No there's not.

Pointing at Marilyn in the white dress serving a table:

That's Marilyn Monroe . . .

Then, pointing at a Blonde Waitress in a tight sweater and capri pants, taking an order from a bunch of film geeks —

. . . and that's Mamie Van Doren. I don't see Jayne Mansfield, so it must be her night off.

Pretty smart.

I have moments.

So, did ya think of something to say?

Actually, there's something I've wanted to ask you about, but you seem like a nice person, and I didn't want to offend you.

Oooohhhh, this doesn't sound like mindless, boring, getting-to-know-you chit-chat. This sounds like you actually have something to say.

Only if you promise not to get offended.

You can't promise something like that. I have no idea what you're gonna ask. You could ask me what you're gonna ask me, and my natural response could be to be offended. Then, through no fault of my own, I would've broken my promise.

Then let's just forget it.

MIA

That is an impossibility. Trying to forget anything as intriguing as this would be an exercise in futility.

VINCENT

Is that a fact?

Mia nods her head: 'Yes.'

MIA

Besides, it's more exciting when you don't have permission.

VINCENT

Well, here goes. What do you think about what happened to Antwan?

MIA

Who's Antwan?

VINCENT

Tony Rocky Horror.

MIA

He fell out of a window.

VINCENT

That's one way to say it. Another way is, he was thrown out. Another way is, he was thrown out by Marsellus. And even another way is, he was thrown out of a window by Marsellus because of you.

MIA

Is that a fact?

VINCENT

No it's not, it's just what I heard.

MIA

Who told you?

VINCENT

They.

Mia and Vincent smile.

MIA

'They' talk a lot, don't they?

VINCENT

They certainly do.

MIA

Well don't be shy, Vincent, what exactly did *they* say?

Vincent is slow to answer.

MIA

Let me help you, Bashful, did it involve the F-word?

VINCENT

No. They just said Rocky Horror gave you a foot massage.

MIA

And . . . ?

VINCENT

No *and*, that's it.

MIA

You heard Marsellus threw Rocky Horror out of a four-story window because he massaged my feet?

VINCENT

Yeah.

MIA

And you believed that?

VINCENT

At the time I was told, it seemed reasonable.

MIA

Marsellus throwing Tony out of a four-story window for giving me a foot massage seemed reasonable?

VINCENT

No, it seemed excessive. But that doesn't mean it didn't happen. I heard Marsellus is very protective of you.

MIA

A husband being protective of his wife is one thing. A husband

62

almost killing another man for touching his wife's feet is something else.

VINCENT

But did it happen?

MIA

The only thing Antwan ever touched of mine was my hand, when he shook it at my wedding. The truth is, nobody knows why Marsellus tossed Tony Rocky Horror out of that window except Marsellus and Tony Rocky Horror. But when you scamps get together, you're worse than a sewing circle.

VINCENT

*[Are you mad?

MIA

Not at all. Being the subject of back-fence gossip goes with the ring, I guess.

She takes a sip of her five-dollar shake, and says:

. . . Thanks.

VINCENT

What for?

MIA

Asking my side.

At that moment, a great oldie-but-goodie blasts from the jukebox.

MIA

I wanna dance.

VINCENT

I'm not much of a dancer.

MIA

Now I'm the one gettin' gypped. I do believe Marsellus told you to take me out and do whatever I wanted. Well, now I want to dance.

* Cut from completed film.

Vincent smiles and begins taking off his boots. Mia triumphantly casts hers off. He takes her hand, escorting her to the dance floor. The two face each other for that brief moment before you begin to dance, then they both break into a devilish twist. Mia's version of the twist is that of a sexy swivelling rhythm that would make Mr Checker proud.

The other dancers on the floor are trying to do the same thing, but Vincent and Mia seem to be strangely shaking their asses in sync. The two definitely share a rhythm and share smiles as they sing along with the last verse of the golden oldie.]

CUT TO:

\[[Ed Sullivan and Marilyn Monroe stand on stage.

ED SULLIVAN
(*into microphone*)
Ladies and gentlemen, now the moment you've all been waiting for, the world-famous Jackrabbit Slim's twist contest.

Patrons cheer.

Ed Sullivan is with Marilyn Monroe, who holds a trophy.

. . . One lucky couple will win this handsome trophy that Marilyn here is holding.

Marilyn holds up the trophy.

. . . Now, who will be our first contestants?

Mia holds up her hand.

MIA
Right here.

Vincent reacts.

I wanna dance.

VINCENT
No, no, no, no, no, no, no, no.

* Added during filming.

64

MIA
(*overlapping*)

No, no, no, no, no, no, no. I do believe Marsellus, my husband,
your boss, told you to take me out and do whatever I wanted.
Now, I want to dance. I want to win. I want that trophy.

VINCENT
(*sighs*)

All right.

MIA

So, dance good.

VINCENT

All right, you asked for it.

Vincent and Mia walk onto the dance floor, toward Ed Sullivan.

ED SULLIVAN
(*into microphone*)

Let's hear it for our first contestants.

Patrons cheer.

Vincent and Mia walk up to the microphone.

. . . Now, let's meet our first contestants here this evening. Young
lady, what is your name?

Mia grabs the microphone.

MIA
(*into microphone*)

Missus Mia Wallace.

ED SULLIVAN
(*into microphone*)

And, uh, how 'bout your fella here?

MIA
(*into microphone*)

Vincent Vega.

ED SULLIVAN
(*into microphone*)
All right, let's see what you can do. Take it away!

Mia and Vincent dance to Chuck Berry's 'You Never Can Tell'. They make hand movements as they dance.]]

INT. MARSELLUS WALLACE'S HOME – NIGHT

The front door flings open, and Mia and Vincent dance tango-style into the house, singing a cappella *the song from the previous scene. They finish their little dance, laughing.*

Then . . .

The two just stand face to face looking at each other.

VINCENT
Was that an uncomfortable silence?

MIA
I don't know what that was.
(*pause*)
Music and drinks!

Mia moves away to attend to both. Vincent hangs up his overcoat on a big bronze coat rack in the alcove.

VINCENT
I'm gonna take a piss.

MIA
That was a little bit more information than I needed to know, but go right ahead.

Vincent shuffles off to the john.

Mia moves to her CD player, thumbs through a stack of CDs and selects one: Urge Overkills 'Girl, You'll Be a Woman Soon.' The speakers blast out a high energy number. Mia dances her way around the room and finds herself by Vincent's overcoat hanging on the rack. She touches its sleeve. It feels good.

Her hand goes into its pocket and pulls out his tobacco pouch. Like a little

67

girl playing cowboy, she spreads the tobacco on some rolling paper.
Imitating what he did earlier, she licks the paper and rolls it into a pretty
good cigarette. Maybe a little too fat, but not bad for a first try. Mia
thinks so anyway. Her hand reaches back into the pocket and pulls out his
Zippo lighter. She slaps the lighter against her leg, trying to light it
fancy-style like Vince did. What do you know, she did it! Mia's one
happy clam. She triumphantly brings the fat flame up to her fat smoke,
lighting it up, then loudly snaps the Zippo closed.

The Mia-made cigarette is brought up to her lips, and she takes a long,
cool drag. Her hand slides the Zippo back in the overcoat pocket. But
wait, her fingers touch something else. Those fingers bring out a plastic
bag with white powder inside, the madman that Vincent bought earlier
from Lance. Wearing a big smile, Mia brings the bag of heroin up to her
face.

                           MIA
                  (like you would say Bingo!)
Disco! Vince, you little cola nut, you've been holding out on me.

    CUT TO:

INT. BATHROOM (MARSELLUS WALLACE'S HOUSE) – NIGHT

Vincent stands at the sink, washing his hands, talking to himself in the
mirror.

                         VINCENT
One drink and that's it. Don't be rude, but drink your drink
quickly, say goodbye, walk out the door, get in your car, and go
down the road.

LIVING ROOM

Mia has the unbeknownst-to-her heroin cut up into big lines on her glass
top coffee table. Taking her trusty hundred dollar bill like a human
Dust-Buster, she quickly snorts the fat line.

CU – MIA
her head jerks back. Her hands go to her nose (which feels like it's on
fucking fire), something is terribly wrong. Then . . . the rush hits . . .

BATHROOM

Vincent dries his hands on a towel while he continues his dialogue with the mirror.

. . . it's a moral test of yourself, whether or not you can maintain loyalty. Because when people are loyal to each other, that's very meaningful.

LIVING ROOM

Mia is on all fours trying to crawl to the bathroom, but it's like she's trying to crawl with the bones removed from her knees. Blood begins to drip from Mia's nose. Then her stomach gets into the act and she vomits.

BATHROOM

Vince continues.

. . . So you're gonna go out there, drink your drink, say 'Goodnight, I've had a very lovely evening,' go home and jack off. And that's all you're gonna do.

Now that he's given himself a little pep talk, Vincent's ready for whatever's waiting for him on the other side of that door. So he goes through it.

LIVING ROOM

We follow behind Vincent as he walks from the bathroom to the living room, where he finds Mia lying on the floor like a rag doll. She's twisted on her back. Blood and puke are down her front. And her face is contorted. Not out of the tightness of pain, but just the opposite, the muscles in her face are so relaxeed, she lies still with her mouth wide open. Slack-jawed.

. . . Jesus Christ

Vincent moves like greased lightning to Mia's fallen body. Bending down where she lays, he puts his fingers on her neck to check her pulse. She slightly stirs.

Mia is aware of Vincent over her, speaking to her.

(sounding weird)
. . . Mia! Mia! What the hell happened?

But she's unable to communicate. Mia makes a few lost mumbles, but they're not distinctive enough to be called words.

Vincent props her eyelids open and sees the story.

(*to himself*)
. . . I'll be a sonofabitch.

(*to Mia*)
Mia! Mia! What did you take? Answer me, honey, what did you take?

Mia is incapable of answering. He slaps her face hard.

Vincent springs up and runs to his overcoat, hanging on the rack. He goes through the pockets frantically. It's gone. Vincent makes a beeline to Mia. We follow.

(*yelling to Mia*)
. . .Okay, honey, we're getting you on your feet.

He reaches her and hoists the dead weight up in his arms.

. . . We're on our feet now, and now we're gonna walk out to the car. Here we go, watch us walk.

We follow behind as he hurriedly walks the practically unconscious Mia through the house and out the front door.

EXT. VINCENT'S HOT ROD (MOVING) – NIGHT

INSERT SPEEDOMETER: *red needle on a hundred. Vincent driving like a madman in a town without traffic laws, speeds the car into turns and up and over hills.*

INT. VINCENT'S HOT ROD (MOVING) – NIGHT

Vincent, one hand firmly on the wheel, the other shifting like Robocop, both eyes staring straight ahead except when he glances over at Mia.

Mia, slack-jawed expression, mouth gaping, posture of a bag of water.

VINCENT
Don't fucking die on me, Mia!

Vincent takes a cellular phone out of his pocket. He punches a number.

Answer!

INT. LANCE'S HOUSE — NIGHT

At this late hour, Lance has transformed from a bon vivant *drug dealer to a bathrobe creature.*

He sits in a big comfy chair, ratty blue gym pants, a worn-out but comfortable T-shirt that has written on it: TAFT, CALIFORNIA and a moth-ridden terry cloth robe. In his hand is a bowl of Cap'n Crunch with Crunch Berries. In front of him on the coffee table is a jug of milk, the box the Cap'n Crunch with Crunch Berries came out of, and a hash pipe in an ashtray.

On the big-screen TV in front of the table is the Three Stooges, and they're getting married.

> PREACHER (EMIL SIMKUS)
> *(on TV)*
>
> Hold hands, you lovebirds

The phone rings.

Lance puts down his cereal and makes his way to the phone.

It rings again.

Jody, his wife, calls from the bedroom, obviously woken up.

> JODY
> *(off)*
>
> Lance! The phone's ringing!

> LANCE
> *(calling back)*
>
> I can hear it!

> JODY
> *(off)*
>
> I thought you told those fuckin' assholes never to call this late!

> LANCE
> *(by the phone)*
>
> I told 'em and that's what I'm gonna tell this fuckin' asshole right now!

(*he answers the phone*)
Hello, do you know how late it is? You're not supposed to be callin' me this fuckin' late.

BACK TO VINCENT IN THE MALIBU

Vincent is still driving like a stripe-assed ape, clutching the phone to his ear. We cut back and forth during the conversation.

> VINCENT
> Lance, this is Vincent, I'm in big fucking trouble man, I'm on my way to your place.

> LANCE
> Whoa, hold your horses man, what's the problem?

> VINCENT
> You still got an adrenalin shot?

> LANCE
> (*dawning on him*)
> Maybe.

> VINCENT
> I need it man, I got a chick she's fuckin' OD'ing on me.

72

LANCE

Don't bring her here! I'm not even fuckin' joking with you, don't you be bringing some fucked up pooh-butt to my house!

VINCENT

No choice.

LANCE

She's OD'in'?

VINCENT

Yeah. She's dyin'.

LANCE

Then bite the fuckin' bullet, take 'er to a hospital and call a lawyer!

VINCENT

Negative.

LANCE

She ain't my fuckin' problem. You fucked her up, you deal with it. Are you talkin' to me on the cellular phone?

VINCENT

Sorry.

LANCE

I don't know you! Who is this? Don't come here, I'm hangin' up.

VINCENT

Too late, I'm already here.

At that moment inside Lance's house we hear Vincent's Malibu coming up the street. Lance hangs up the phone, goes to his curtains and yanks the cord. The curtains open with a WHOOSH *in time to see Vincent's Malibu driving up on his front lawn and crashing into his house. The window Lance is looking out of shatters from the impact.*

JODY
(off)

What the hell was that?

Lance charges from the window, out the door to his front lawn.

Vincent is already out of the car, working on getting Mia out.

> LANCE

Have you lost your mind? You crashed your car in my fuckin' house! You talk about drug shit on a cellular fuckin' phone —

> VINCENT

If you're through havin' your little hissy fit, this chick is dyin', get your needle and git it now!

> LANCE

Are you deaf? You're not bringin' that fucked up bitch in my house!

> VINCENT

This fucked up bitch is Marsellus Wallace's wife. Do you know who Marsellus Wallace is? Do you?

> LANCE

Yeah. Yeah.

> VINCENT

Now if she fuckin' croaks on me, I'm a grease spot. But before he turns me into a bar of soap, I'm gonna be forced to tell 'im about how you coulda saved her life, but instead you let her die on your front lawn. Now, come on, help me, help me. Pick her up.

Vincent and Lance pick up Mia and carry her towards the house.

INT. LANCE'S HOUSE — NIGHT

We start in Lance's and Jody's bedroom.

Jody, in bed, throws off the covers and stands up. She's wearing a long T-shirt with a picture of Fred Flintstone on it.

We follow handheld behind her as she opens the door, walking through the hall into the living room.

> JODY

Lance! It's only one-thirty in the goddamn mornin'! What the fuck's goin' on out here?!

As she walks in the living room, she sees Vincent and Lance standing over Mia, who's lying on the floor in the middle of the room.

From here on in, everything in this scene is frantic, like a documentary in an emergency ward, with the big difference here being nobody knows what the fuck they're doing.

> JODY

Who's she?

Lance looks up at Jody.

> LANCE

Go to the fridge and get the thing with the adrenalin shot.

> JODY

What's wrong with her?

> VINCENT

She's OD'ing on us.

> JODY

Well get her the hell outta here!

> LANCE AND VINCENT
> (*in stereo*)

Get the fuckin' shot!

> JODY

Don't yell at me!

She angrily turns and disappears into the kitchen looking for the shot in the fridge.

We move into the room with the two men.

> VINCENT
> (*to Lance*)

You two are a match made in heaven.

> LANCE

Look, just keep talkin' to her, okay? While she's gettin' the shot, I gotta get a medical book.

> VINCENT

What do you need a medical book for?

LANCE

To tell me how to do it. I've never given an adrenalin shot before.

VINCENT

You've had that thing for six years and you never used it?

LANCE

I never had to use it. I don't go joy-poppin' with bubble-gummers. My friends can handle their highs!

VINCENT

Well, then get it.

LANCE

I am, if you'll let me.

VINCENT

I'm not fuckin' stoppin' you.

LANCE

Stop talkin' to me, and start talkin' to her.

We follow Lance as he runs out of the living room into a . . .

SPARE ROOM

with a bunch of junk in it. He frantically starts scanning the junk for the book he's looking for, repeating the words 'Come on' endlessly.

From off screen we hear:

VINCENT
(*off*)

Hurry up man! We're losin' her!

LANCE
(*calling back*)

I'm looking as fast as I can!

Lance continues his frenzied search.

We hear Jody in the living room now as she talks to Vincent.

JODY
(*off*)

What's he lookin' for?

VINCENT
(*off*)

I dunno, some medical book.

Jody calls to Lance.

JODY
(*off*)

What are you lookin' for?

LANCE

My black medical book!

As he continues searching, flipping and knocking over shit, Jody appears in the doorway.

JODY

What are you looking for?

LANCE

My black fuckin' medical book. It's like a textbook they give to nurses.

JODY

I never saw a medical book.

LANCE

Trust me, I have one.

JODY

Well, if it's that important, why didn't you keep it with the shot?

Lance spins towards her.

LANCE

I don't know. Stop bothering me!

JODY

While you're lookin' for it, that girl's gonna die on our carpet. You're never gonna find it in all this shit. For six months now, I've been tellin' you to clean this room –

LANCE

Honey, I'm going to fuckin' kill you if you don't shut up.

VINCENT
(*off*)

Get your ass in here, fuck the book!

Lance angrily knocks over a pile of shit and leaves the shot heading for the living room.

LIVING ROOM

Vincent is bent over Mia, talking softly to her, when Lance reenters the room.

VINCENT

Quit fuckin' around man and give her the shot!

Lance bends down by the black case brought in by Jody. He opens it and begins preparing the needle for the injection.

LANCE

While I'm doing this, take her shirt off and find her heart.

Vincent rips the blouse open.

Jody stumbles back in the room, hanging back from the action.

VINCENT

Does it have to be exact?

LANCE

Yeah, it has to be exact! I'm giving her an injection in the heart, so I guess it's gotta be fuckin' exact.

VINCENT

Well, I don't know exactly where her heart is. I think it's here.

Vince points to Mia's right breast. Lance glances over and nods.

LANCE

That's it.

As Lance readies the injection, Vincent looks up at Jody.

VINCENT

I need a big fat magic marker. Got one?

JODY

What?

VINCENT

I need a big fat magic marker, any felt pen'll do, but a magic marker would be great.

JODY

Hold on.

Jody runs to the desk, opens the top drawer and, in her enthusiasm, she pulls the drawer out of the desk, the contents of which (bills, papers, pens) spill to the floor.

The injection is ready. Lance hands Vincent the needle.

LANCE

It's ready, I'll tell you what to do.

VINCENT

No, no, no, no. You're gonna give her the shot.

LANCE

No, you're gonna give her the shot.

VINCENT

I've never done this before.

LANCE

I've never done this before either, and I ain't startin' now. You brought 'er here, that means you give her the shot. The day I bring an OD'ing bitch to your place, then I gotta give her the shot.

Jody hurriedly joins them in the huddle, a big fat red magic marker in her hand.

JODY

Got it.

Vincent grabs the magic marker out of Jody's hand and makes a big red dot on Mia's body where her heart is.

VINCENT

Okay, what do I do?

LANCE

Well, you're giving her an injection of adrenalin straight to her heart. But she's got a breastplate in front of her heart, so you gotta pierce through that. So what you gotta do is bring the needle down in a stabbing motion.

Lance demonstrates a stabbing motion, which looks like 'The Shape' killing its victims in Halloween.

                              VINCENT
I gotta stab her?

                              LANCE
If you want the needle to pierce through to her heart, you gotta stab her hard. Then once you do, push down the plunger.

                              VINCENT
What happens after that?

                              LANCE
I'm curious about that myself.

                              VINCENT
This ain't a fuckin' joke, man!

                              LANCE
She's supposed to come out of it like –

(*snaps his fingers*)

– that.

Vincent lifts the needle up above his head in a stabbing motion. He looks down on Mia.

Mia is fading fast. Soon nothing will help her.

Vincent's eyes narrow, ready to do this.

                              VINCENT
Count to three.

Lance, on his knees right beside Vincent, does not know what to expect.

                              LANCE
One . . .

Red dot on Mia's body.

Needle raised ready to strike.

. . . Two . . .

Jody's face is alive with anticipation.

Needle in the air, poised like a rattler ready to strike.

. . . three!

The needle leaves the frame, thrusting down hard.

Vincent brings the needle down hard, stabbing Mia in the chest.

Mia's head is jolted from the impact.

The syringe plunger is pushed down, pumping the adrenalin out through the needle.

Mia's eyes pop wide open and she lets out a hellish cry of the banshee. She bolts up in a sitting position, needle stuck in her chest – screaming.

Vincent, Lance and Jody, who were in sitting positions in front of Mia, jump back, scared to death.

Mia's scream runs out. She slowly starts taking breaths of air.

The other three, now scooted halfway across the room, shaken to their bones, look to see if she's alright.

LANCE
If you're okay, say something.

Mia, still breathing, not looking up at them, says in a relatively normal voice:

MIA
Something.

Vincent and Lance collapse on their backs, exhausted and shaking from how close to death Mia came.

JODY
Anybody want a beer?

CUT TO.

INT. VINCENT'S MALIBU (MOVING) – NIGHT

Vincent is behind the wheel driving Mia home. No one says anything, both are still too shaken.

EXT. FRONT OF MARSELLUS WALLACE'S HOUSE – NIGHT

The Malibu pulls up to the front. Mia gets out without saying a word (still in a daze) and begins walking down the walkway toward her front door.

> VINCENT
> *(off)*

Mia!

She turns around.

Vincent's out of the car, standing on the walkway, a big distance between the two.

What are your thoughts on how to handle this?

> MIA

What's yours?

> VINCENT

Well, I'm of the opinion that Marsellus can live his whole life and never ever hear of this incident.

Mia smiles.

> MIA

Don't worry about it. If Marsellus ever heard of this, I'd be in as much trouble as you.

> VINCENT

I seriously doubt that.

> MIA

If you can keep a secret, so can I.

> VINCENT

Let's shake on it.

They walk toward each other, holding out their hands to shake and shake they do.

Mum's the word.

Mia lets go of Vincent's hand and silently makes the see-no-evil, hear-no-evil, and speak-no-evil sign with her hands.

Vincent smiles.

VINCENT

If you'll excuse me, I gotta go home and have a heart attack.

Mia giggles.

Vincent turns to leave.

MIA

Vincent! You still wanna hear my 'Fox Force Five' joke?

Vincent turns round.

VINCENT

Sure, but I think I'm still a little too petrified to laugh.

MIA

Uh-huh. You won't laugh because it's not funny. But if you still wanna hear it, I'll tell it.

VINCENT

I can't wait.

MIA

Okay. Three tomatoes are walking down the street, a poppa tomato, a momma tomato and a little baby tomato. The baby tomato is lagging behind the poppa and momma tomato. The poppa tomato gets mad, goes over to the baby tomato and stamps on him –

(*stamps the ground*)

– and says: 'catch up.'

They both smile, but neither laughs.

MIA

See ya 'round, Vince.

Mia turns and walks inside her house.

CU — VINCENT

after Mia walks inside. Vincent continues to look at where she was. He brings his hands to his lips and blows her a kiss. Then exits frame leaving it empty. We hear his Malibu start up and drive away.

FADE TO BLACK

FADE UP:

On the cartoon 'Speed Racer.' Speed is giving a detailed description of all the features on his race car 'The Mac-5,' which he does at the beginning of every episode.

Off screen we hear a woman's voice . . .

> WOMAN'S VOICE
> (*off*)

Butch.

DISSOLVE TO:

BUTCH'S POV

We're in the living room of a modest two bedroom house in Alhambra, California, in the year 1972. Butch's Mother, thirty-five-ish, stands in the doorway leading into the living room. Next to her is a man dressed in the uniform of an American Air Force officer. The camera is the perspective of a 5-year-old boy.

> MOTHER

Butch, stop watching TV a second. We got a special visitor. Now do you remember when I told you your daddy died in a POW camp?

> BUTCH
> (*off*)

Uh-huh.

> MOTHER

Well this here is Captain Koons. He was in the POW camp with Daddy.

Captain Koons steps inside the room toward the little boy and bends down on one knee to bring him even with the boy's eyeline. When Koons speaks, he speaks with a slight Texas accent.

CAPTAIN KOONS

Hello, little man. Boy, I sure heard a bunch about you. See, I was a good friend of your Daddy's. We were in that Hanoi pit of hell over five years together. Hopefully, you'll never have to experience this yourself, but when two men are in a situation like me and your Daddy were, for as long as we were, you take on certain responsibilities for the other. If it had been me who had not made it, Major Coolidge would be talkin' right now to my son Jim. But the way it worked out is I'm talkin' to you, Butch. I got somethin' for ya.

The Captain pulls a gold wristwatch out of his pocket.

. . . This watch I got here was first purchased by your great-granddaddy. It was bought during the First World War in a little general store in Knoxville, Tennessee. It was bought by private Doughboy Ernie Coolidge the day he set sail for Paris. It was your great-granddaddy's war watch, made by the first company ever to make wristwatches. You see, up until then, people just carried pocket watches. Your great-granddaddy wore that watch every day he was in the war. Then when he had done his duty, he went home to your great-grandmother, took the watch off his wrist and put it in an ol' coffee can. And in that can it stayed 'til your

grandfather Dane Coolidge was called upon by his country to go
overseas and fight the Germans once again. This time they called it
World War Two. Your great-granddaddy gave it to your granddad
for good luck. Unfortunately. Dane's luck wasn't as good as his
old man's. Your granddad was a Marine and he was killed with all
the other Marines at the battle of Wake Island. Your granddad
was facing death and he knew it. None of the boys had any
illusions about ever leavin' that island alive. So three days before
the Japanese took the island, your 22-year-old grandfather asked a
gunner on an Air Force transport named Winocki, a man he had
never met before in his life, to deliver to his infant son, who he
had never seen in the flesh, his gold watch. Three days later, your
grandfather was dead. But Winocki kept his word. After the war
was over, he paid a visit to your grandmother, delivering to your
infant father his Dad's gold watch. This watch. This watch was
on your Daddy's wrist when he was shot down over Hanoi. He
was captured and put in a Vietnamese prison camp. Now he knew
if the gooks ever saw the watch it'd be confiscated. The way your
Daddy looked at it, that watch was your birthright. And he'd be
damned if any slopeheads were gonna put their greasy yella hands
on his boy's birthright. So he hid it in the one place he knew he
could hide somethin'. His ass. Five long years, he wore this watch
up his ass. Then when he died of dysentery, he gave me the watch,
I hid this uncomfortable hunk of metal up my ass for two years.
Then, after seven years, I was sent home to my family. And now,
little man, I give the watch to you.

*Captain Koons hands the watch to Butch. A little hand comes into frame
to accept it.*

CUT TO:

INT. LOCKER ROOM – NIGHT

*The 27-year-old Butch Coolidge is dressed in boxing regalia: trunks,
shoes and gloves. He lies on a table catching a few zzzzzz's before his big
fight. Almost as soon as we cut to him, he wakes up with a start. Shaken
by the bizarre memory, he wipes his sweaty face with his boxing glove.*

His trainer Klondike, an older fireplug, opens the door a little, sticking his

head in the room. *Pandemonium seems to be breaking out behind
Klondike in the hallway.*

KLONDIKE

It's time, Butch.

BUTCH

I'm ready.

*Klondike steps inside, closing the door on the wild mob outside. He goes to
the long yellow robe hanging on a hook. Butch hops off the table and,
without a word, Klondike helps him on with the robe, which says on the
back:* BATTLING BUTCH COOLIDGE.

*The two men head for the door. Klondike opens the door for Butch. As
Butch steps into the hallway, the crowd goes apeshit. Klondike closes the
door behind him, leaving us in the quiet, empty locker room.*

FADE TO BLACK

TITLE CARD:

'THE GOLD WATCH'

WE HEAR OVER THE BLACK AND TITLE:

> SPORTSCASTER #1
> (*off*)

— Well, Dan, that had to be the bloodiest and, hands-down, the most brutal fight this city has ever seen.

The sound of chaos in the background.

FADE IN:

EXT. ALLEY (RAINING) — NIGHT

A taxi is parked in a dark alley next to an auditorium. The sky is pissin' down rain. We slowly dolly toward the parked car. The sound of the car radio can be heard coming from inside.

. . . Coolidge was out of there faster than I've ever seen a victorious boxer vacate the ring. Do you think he knew Willis was dead?

> SPORTSCASTER #2
> (*off*)

My guess would be yes, Richard. I could see from my position here, the frenzy in his eyes gave way to the realization of what he was doing. I think any man would've left the ring that fast.

DISSOLVE TO:

INT. TAXI (PARKED/RAINING) — NIGHT

Inside the taxi, behind the wheel, is a female cabbie named Esmarelda Villalobos. A young woman, with Spanish looks, sits parked, drinking a steaming hot cup of coffee out of a white styrofoam cup.

The sportscasters continue their coverage.

> SPORTSCASTER #1

Do you feel this ring death tragedy will have an effect on the world of boxing?

Oh Dan, a tragedy like this can't help but shake the world of boxing to its very foundation. But it's of paramount importance that during the sad weeks ahead, the eyes of the WBA remain firmly fixed on the – CLICK –

Esmarelda shuts off the radio.

She takes a sip of coffee, then hears a noise behind her in the alley. She sticks her head out of the car door to see:

A window about three stories high opens on the auditorium-side of the alley. A gym bag is tossed out into a garbage dumpster below the window. Then, Butch Coolidge, still dressed in boxing trunks, shoes, gloves and yellow robe, leaps to the dumpster below.

Esmarelda's reaction takes in the strangeness of this sight.

Gym bag in hand, Butch climbs out of the dumpster and runs to the taxi. Before he climbs in, he takes off his robe and throws it to the ground.

INT. TAXI (PARKED/RAINING) – NIGHT

Butch, soaking wet, naked except for trunks, shoes and gloves, hops in the back seat, slamming the door.

Esmarelda, staring straight ahead, talks to Butch through the rearview mirror:

ESMARELDA
(*Spanish accent*)
Are you the man I was supposed to pick up?

BUTCH
If you're the cab I called, I'm the guy you're supposed to pick up.

ESMARELDA
Where to?

BUTCH
Outta here.

The ignition key is twisted. The engine roars to life.

The meter is flipped on.

Esmarelda's bare foot stomps on the gas pedal.

89

EXT. BOXING AUDITORIUM (RAINING) – NIGHT

The cab whips out of the alley, fish-tailing on the wet pavement in front of the auditorium at a rapid pace.

INT. WILLIS LOCKER ROOM (AUDITORIUM) – NIGHT

Locker-room door opens, English Dave fights his way through the pandemonium which is going on outside the hall, shutting the door on the madness. Once inside, English Dave takes time to adjust his suit and tie.
*[[Mia is standing by the door. She sees Vincent with English Dave.

> VINCENT
> Mia. How you doin'?

> MIA
> Great. I never thanked you for dinner.]]

In the room, black boxer Floyd Ray Willis lies on a table – dead. His face looks like he went dunking for bees. His trainer is on his knees, head on Floyd's chest, crying over the body.

* Added during filming.

The huge figure that is Marsellus Wallace stands at the table, hands on the trainer's shoulder, lending emotional support. We still do not see Marsellus clearly, only that he is big.

Mia sits in a chair at the far end of the room.

Marsellus looks up, sees English Dave and walks over to him.

> MARSELLUS
> (*off*)
>
> What'cha got?

> ENGLISH DAVE
>
> He booked.

> MARSELLUS
> (*off*)
>
> I'm prepared to scour the earth for this motherfucker. If Butch goes to Indo-China, I want a nigger hidin' in a bowl of rice, ready to pop a cap in his ass.

> ENGLISH DAVE
>
> I'll take care of it.

INT. CAB (MOVING/RAINING) – NIGHT

Butch gets one of his boxing gloves off.

Esmarelda watches in the rearview mirror.

He tries to roll down one of the back-seat windows, but can't find the roll bar.

> BUTCH
>
> Hey, how do I open the window back here?

> ESMARELDA
>
> I have to do it.

She presses a button and the back window moves down. Butch tosses his boxing glove out the window, then starts untying the other one.

Esmarelda can't keep quiet anymore.

> ESMARELDA
>
> Hey, mister?

BUTCH
(*still working on the glove*)

What?

ESMARELDA

You were in that fight? The fight on the radio – you're the fighter?

As he tosses his other glove out the window.

BUTCH

Whatever gave you that idea?

ESMARELDA

No c'mon, you're him, I know you're him, tell me you're him.

BUTCH
(*drying himself with a gym towel*)

I'm him.

ESMARELDA

You killed the other boxing man.

BUTCH

He's dead?

ESMARELDA

The radio said he was dead.

He finishes wiping himself down.

BUTCH
(*to himself*)

Sorry 'bout that, Floyd.

He tosses the towel out the window.

Silence as Butch digs in his bag for a T-shirt.

ESMARELDA

What does it feel like?

BUTCH
(*finds his shirt*)

What does what feel like?

ESMARELDA

Killing a man. Beating another man to death with your bare hands.

Butch pulls on his T-shirt.

BUTCH

Are you some kinda weirdo?

ESMARELDA

No, it's a subject I have much interest in. You are the first person I ever met who has killed somebody. So, what was it like to kill a man?

BUTCH

Tell ya what, you give me one of them cigarettes, I'll give you an answer.

Esmarelda bounces in her seat with excitement.

ESMARELDA

Deal!

Butch leans forward. Esmarelda, keeping her eyes on the road, passes a cigarette back to him. He takes it. Then, still not looking behind her, she brings up her hand, a lit match in it. Butch lights his smoke, then blows out the match.

He takes a long drag.

BUTCH

So . . .

He looks at her license.

. . . Esmarelda Villalobos – is that Mexican?

ESMARELDA

The name is Spanish, but I'm Colombian.

BUTCH

It's a very pretty name.

ESMARELDA

It means 'Esmarelda of the wolves'.

BUTCH

That's one hell of a name you got there, sister.

ESMARELDA

Thank you. And what is your name?

BUTCH

Butch.

ESMARELDA

Butch. What does it mean?

BUTCH

I'm an American, our names don't mean shit. Anyway, moving right along, what is it you wanna know, Esmarelda?

ESMARELDA

I want to know what it feels like to kill a man –

BUTCH

– I couldn't tell ya. I didn't know he was dead. Now I know he's dead, do you wanna know how I feel about it?

Esmarelda nods her head: 'Yes.'

BUTCH

I don't feel the least little bit bad. *[You wanna know why, Esmarelda?

Esmarelda nods her head: 'Yes.'

. . . 'Cause I'm a boxer. And after you've said that, you've said pretty much all there is to say about me. Now maybe that son-of-a-bitch tonight was once at one time a boxer. If he was, then he was dead before his ass ever stepped in the ring. I just put the poor bastard outta his misery. And if he never was a boxer –

(*Butch takes a drag*)

That's what he gets for fuckin' up my my sport.]

---

* Cut from completed film.

We dolly around a phone booth as Butch talks inside.

> BUTCH
> (*into the phone*)
> What'd I tell ya, soon as the word got out a fix was in, the odds
> went through the roof. Hey, if he was a better fighter he'd be
> alive. If he never laced up his gloves in the first place, which he
> never shoulda done, he'd be alive. Enough about the poor
> unfortunate Mr Floyd, let's talk about the rich and prosperous Mr
> Butch. How many bookies you spread it around with?
> (*pause*)
> Eight? How long to collect?
> (*pause*)
> So by tomorrow evening, you'll have it all?
> (*pause*)
> Good news, Scotty, real good news – I understand, a few
> stragglers aside. Me an' Fabienne're gonna leave in the morning.
> It should take us a couple of days to get into Knoxville. Next time
> we see each other, it'll be on Tennessee time.

Butch hangs up the phone. He looks at the cab waiting to take him wherever he wants to go.

> (*to himself in French with English subtitles*)
> Fabienne my love, our adventure begins.

CUT TO:

EXT. MOTEL (STOPPED RAINING) – NIGHT

Esmarelda's taxi pulls into the motel parking lot. The rain has stopped, but the night is still soaked. Butch gets out, now fully dressed in T-shirt, jeans and high-school athletic jacket. He leans in the driver's side window.

> ESMARELDA
> Forty-five sixty.

Handing her the money.

BUTCH

Merci beaucoup. And here's a little something for the effort.

Butch holds up a hundred-dollar bill.

Esmarelda's eyes light up. She goes to take it. Butch holds it out of reach.

BUTCH

Now if anybody should ask you about who your fare was tonight, what're you gonna tell 'em?

ESMARELDA

The truth. Three well-dressed, slightly toasted Mexicans.

He gives her the bill.

BUTCH

Bon soir, Esmarelda.

ESMARELDA
(*in Spanish*)

Sleep well, Butch.

He tweaks her nose, she smiles, and he turns and walks away. She drives off.

INT. MOTEL (ROOM 6) – NIGHT

Butch enters and turns on the light.

Lying curled up on the bed, fully dressed, with her back to us is Butch's French girlfriend, Fabienne.

FABIENNE

Keep the light off.

Butch flicks the switch back, making the room dark again.

BUTCH

Is that better, sugar pop?

FABIENNE

Oui. Hard day at the office?

BUTCH

Pretty hard. I got into a fight.

FABIENNE

Poor baby. Can we make spoons?

Butch climbs into bed, spooning Fabienne from behind.

When Butch and Fabienne speak to each other, they speak in baby talk.

FABIENNE

I was looking at myself in the mirror.

BUTCH

Uh-huh?

FABIENNE

I wish I had a pot.

BUTCH

You were lookin' in the mirror and you wish you had some pot?

FABIENNE

A pot. A potbelly. Potbellies are sexy.

BUTCH

Well you should be happy, 'cause you do.

FABIENNE

Shut up, Fatso! I don't have a pot! I have a bit of a tummy, like
Madonna when she did 'Lucky Star.' It's not the same thing.

BUTCH

I didn't realize there was a difference between a tummy and a
potbelly.

FABIENNE

The difference is huge.

BUTCH

You want me to have a pot?

FABIENNE

No. Potbellies make a man look either oafish or like a gorilla. But
on a woman, a potbelly is very sexy. The rest of you is normal.
Normal face, normal legs, normal hips, normal ass, but with a big,
perfectly round potbelly. If I had one, I'd wear a T-shirt two sizes
too small to accentuate it.

BUTCH

You think guys would find that attractive?

FABIENNE

I don't give a damn what men find attractive. It's unfortunate
what we find pleasing to the touch and pleasing to the eye is
seldom the same.

BUTCH

If you had a potbelly, I'd punch you in it.

FABIENNE

You'd punch me in my belly?

BUTCH

Right in the belly.

FABIENNE

I'd smother you. I'd drop it on you right on your face 'til you
couldn't breathe.

BUTCH

You'd do that to me?

FABIENNE

Yes!

BUTCH

Did you get everything, sugar pop?

FABIENNE

Yes, I did.

BUTCH

Good job.

FABIENNE

Did everything go as planned?

BUTCH

You didn't listen to the radio?

FABIENNE

I never listen to your fights. Were you the winner?

BUTCH

I won alright.

FABIENNE

Are you still retiring?

BUTCH

Sure am.

FABIENNE

What about the man you fought?

BUTCH

Floyd retired too.

FABIENNE
(*smiling*)

Really?! He won't be fighting no more?!

BUTCH

Not no more.

FABIENNE

So it all worked out in the finish?

BUTCH

We ain't at the finish yet, baby.

Fabienne rolls over and Butch gets on top of her. They kiss.

FABIENNE

We're in a lot of danger, aren't we?

Butch nods his head: 'Yes.'

. . . If they find us, they'll kill us, won't they?

Butch nods his head: 'Yes.'

. . .But they won't find us, will they?

Butch nods his head: 'No.'

. . .Do you still want me to go with you?

Butch nods his head: 'Yes.'

. . .I don't want to be a burden or a nuisance –

Butch's hand goes out of frame and starts massaging her crotch.

Fabienne reacts.
. . .Say it!

BUTCH

Fabienne, I want you to be with me.

FABIENNE

Forever?

BUTCH

. . . and ever.

Fabienne lies her head back.

Butch continues to massage her crotch.

FABIENNE

Do you love me?

BUTCH

Oui.

FABIENNE

Butch? Will you give me oral pleasure?

Butch kisses her on the mouth.

BUTCH

Will you kiss it?

She nods her head: 'Yes.'

FABIENNE

But you first.

Butch's head goes down out of frame to carry out the oral pleasure. Fabienne's face is alone in the frame.

(*in French, with English subtitles*)

. . .Butch, my love, the adventure begins.

FADE TO BLACK

FADE UP:

MOTEL ROOM

Same motel room, except empty. We hear the shower running in the bathroom. The camera moves to the bathroom doorway. We see Fabrienne in a white terry cloth robe that seems to swallow her up. She's drying her head with a towel. Butch is inside the shower washing up. We see the outline of his naked body through the smoky glass of the shower door. Steam fills the bathroom. Butch turns the shower off and opens the door, popping his head out.

BUTCH

I think I cracked a rib.

FABIENNE

Giving me oral pleasure?

BUTCH

No, retard, from the fight.

FABIENNE

Don't call me retard.

BUTCH
(*in a Mongoloid voice*)
My name is Fabby! My name is Fabby!

FABIENNE
Shut up, fuck head! I hate that Mongoloid voice.

BUTCH
Okay, sorry, sorry, sorry, I take it back! Can I have a towel please, Miss Beautiful Tulip.

FABIENNE
Oh I like that, I like being called a tulip. Tulip is much better than Mongoloid.

She finishes drying her hair and wraps the towel like a turban on her head.

BUTCH
I didn't call you a Mongoloid, I called you a retard, but I took it back.

She hands him a towel.

Merci beaucoup.

FABIENNE
Butch?

BUTCH
(*drying his head*)
Yes, lemon pie.

FABIENNE
Where are we going to go?

BUTCH
I'm not sure yet. Wherever you want. We're gonna get a lot of money from this. But it ain't gonna be so much, we can live like hogs in the fat house forever. I was thinking we could go somewhere in the South Pacific. The kinda money we'll have'll carry us a long way down there.

FABIENNE
So if we wanted, we could live in Bora Bora?

BUTCH

You betcha. And if after awhile you don't dig Bora Bora, then we can move over to Tahiti or Mexico.

FABIENNE

But I do not speak Spanish.

BUTCH

You don't speak Bora Boran either. Besides, Mexican is easy: *Donde esta el zapataria?*

FABIENNE

What does that mean?

BUTCH

Where's the shoe store?

FABIENNE

Donde esta el zapataria?

BUTCH

Excellent pronunciation. You'll be my little *mama cita* in no time.

Butch exits the bathroom. We stay on Fabienne as she brushes her teeth. Butch keeps on from the other room.

BUTCH
(off)

Que hora es?

FABIENNE

Que hora es?

BUTCH
(off)

What time is it?

FABIENNE

What time is it?

BUTCH
(off)

Time for bed. Sweet dreams, jellybean.

Fabienne brushes her teeth. We watch her for a moment or two, then she remembers something.

Butch.

She walks out of the bathroom to ask Butch a question, only to find him sound asleep in bed.

She looks at him a moment.

. . . Forget it.

She exits frame, going back in the bathroom. We stay on the wide shot of the unconscious Butch in bed.

FADE TO BLACK

FADE UP:

MOTEL ROOM — MORNING

Same shot as before, the next morning. We find Butch still asleep in bed.

Fabienne brushes her teeth half in and half out of the bathroom so she can watch TV at the same time. She still wears the terry cloth robe from the night before.

On TV: William Smith and a bunch of Hell's Angels are taking on the entire Vietnamese army in the film The Losers.

Butch wakes from his sleep, as if a scary monster was chasing him. His start startles Fabienne.

FABIENNE

Merde! You startled me. Did you have a bad dream?

Butch squints down the front of the bed at her, trying to focus.

*[BUTCH

. . . Yeah . . . are you still brushing your teeth?

FABIENNE

This is me. I brush my teeth all night long and into the early morning. Do you think I have a problem?

Fabienne goes back into the bathroom to spit.

* Cut from completed film.

If that was supposed to be sarcasm, it was lost on Butch at this early hour.]

Butch, still trying to chase the cobwebs away, sees on TV Hell's Angels tear-assin' through a Vietnamese prison camp.

BUTCH

What are you watching?

FABIENNE
(off)

A motorcycle movie, I'm not sure the name.

BUTCH

Are you watchin' it?

Fabienne reenters the room.

FABIENNE

In a way. Why? Would you like for me to switch it off?

BUTCH

Would you please?

She reaches over and turns off the TV.

It's a little early in the morning for explosions and war.

FABIENNE

What was it about?

BUTCH

How should I know, you were the one watchin' it.

Fabienne laughs.

FABIENNE

No, imbecile, what was your dream about?

BUTCH

Oh, I . . . don't remember. It's really rare I remember a dream.

*[FABIENNE

You just woke up from it.

* Cut from completed film.

BUTCH

Fabienne, I'm not lying to you, I don't remember.

FABIENNE

Well, let's look at the grumpy man in the morning. I didn't say you were lying, it's just odd you don't remember your dreams. I always remember mine. Did you know you talk in your sleep?

BUTCH

I don't talk in my sleep, do I talk in my sleep?

FABIENNE

You did last night.

BUTCH

What did I say?

Laying on top of him:

FABIENNE

I don't know. I couldn't understand you.]

She kisses Butch.

. . . Why don't you get up and we'll get some breakfast at that breakfast place with the pancakes.

BUTCH

One more kiss and I'll get up.

Fabienne gives Butch a sweet long kiss.

FABIENNE

Satisfied?

BUTCH

Yep.

FABIENNE

Then get up, lazy bones.

Butch climbs out of bed and starts pulling clothes out of the suitcase that Fabienne brought.

BUTCH

What time is it?

FABIENNE
Almost nine in the morning. What time does our train arrive?

BUTCH
Eleven.

*[*Seeing him looking at a pair of pants:*

FABIENNE
Those pants are very nice. Can you wear those with that nice blue shirt you have?

He pulls a blue shirt out of the suitcase.

BUTCH
This one?

FABIENNE
That's the one. That matches.

BUTCH
Okay.

He puts the clothes on.]

FABIENNE
I'm gonna order a big plate of blueberry pancakes with maple syrup, eggs over easy and five sausages.

BUTCH
(*surprised at her potential appetite*)
Anything to drink with that?

Butch is finished dressing.

FABIENNE
(*referring to his clothes*)
Oh yes, that looks nice, to drink, a tall glass of orange juice and a black cup of coffee. After that, I'm going to have a slice of pie.

As he goes through the suitcases.

BUTCH
Pie for breakfast?

* Cut from completed film.

FABIENNE

Any time of the day is a good time for pie. Blueberry pie to go with the pancakes. And on top, a thin slice of melted cheese –

BUTCH

– where's my watch?

FABIENNE

It's there.

BUTCH

No, it's not. It's not here.

FABIENNE

Have you looked?

By now, Butch is frantically rummaging through the suitcases.

BUTCH

Yes, I've fuckin' looked!!

He's now throwing clothes.

What the fuck do you think I'm doing?! Are you sure you got it?

Fabienne can hardly speak, she's never seen Butch this way.

FABIENNE

Uhhh . . . yes . . . beside the table drawer –

BUTCH

– on the little kangaroo.

FABIENNE

Yes, it was on your little kangaroo.

BUTCH

Well, it's not here!

FABIENNE
(*on the verge of tears*)

Well, it should be!

BUTCH

Oh, it most definitely should be here, but it's not. So where is it?

Fabienne is crying and scared.

Butch lowers his voice, which only serves to make him more menacing.

. . . Fabienne, that was my father's fuckin' watch. You know what my father went through to get me that watch? . . . I don't wanna get into it right now . . . but he went through a lot. Now all this other shit, you coulda set on fire, but I specifically reminded you not to forget my father's watch. Now think, did you get it?

> FABIENNE

I believe so. . . .

> BUTCH

You believe so? You either did, or you didn't. Now which one is it?

> FABIENNE

Then I did.

> BUTCH

Are you sure?

> FABIENNE
> (*shaking*)

No.

Butch freaks out, he punches the air.

Fabienne screams and backs into a corner.

Butch picks up the motel TV and throws it against the wall.

Fabienne screams in horror.

Butch looks toward her, suddenly calm.

> BUTCH
> (*to Fabienne*)

No! It's not your fault.
> (*he approaches her*)

You left it at the apartment.

He bends down in front of the woman who has sunk to the floor.

He touches her hand, she flinches.

. . . If you did leave it at the apartment, it's not your fault. I had you bring a bunch of stuff. I reminded you about it, but I didn't illustrate how personal the watch was to me. If all I gave a fuck about was my watch, I should've told you. You're not a mind reader.

He kisses her hand. Then rises.

Fabienne is still sniffling.

Butch goes to the closet.

FABIENNE

I'm sorry.

Butch puts on his high-school jacket.

BUTCH

Don't be. It just means I won't be able to eat breakfast with you.

FABIENNE

Why does it mean that?

BUTCH

Because I'm going back to my apartment to get my watch.

FABIENNE

Won't the gangsters be looking for you there?

BUTCH

That's what I'm gonna find out. If they are, and I don't think I can handle it, I'll split.

Rising from the floor:

*[FABIENNE

My darling, I don't want you to be murdered over a silly watch.

BUTCH

One, it's not a silly watch. Two, I'm not gonna be murdered. And three, don't be scared. I won't let anything get in the way of us living a happy life together.

FABIENNE

What about our train?

BUTCH

We gotta couple hours yet.]

FABIENNE

I feel so dreadful. I saw your watch, I thought I brought it. I'm so sorry.

Butch brings her close and puts his hands on her face.

BUTCH

Don't feel bad, sugar pop. Nothing you could ever do would make me permanently angry at you.
                    (*pause*)
I love you, remember?
                    (*he digs some money out of his wallet*)
Now here's some money, order those pancakes and have a great breakfast.

FABIENNE

Don't go.

---

* Cut from completed film.

BUTCH

I'll be back before you can say blueberry pie.

FABIENNE

Blueberry pie.

BUTCH

Well maybe not that fast, but fast. Okay? Okay?

FABIENNE

Okay.

He kisses her once more and heads for the door.

BUTCH

Bye-bye, sugar pop.

FABIENNE

Bye.

BUTCH

I'm gonna take your Honda.

FABIENNE

Okay.

And with that, he's out the door.

Fabienne sits on the bed and looks at the money he gave her.

INT. HONDA (MOVING) – DAY

Butch is beating the steering wheel and the dash with his fists as he drives down the street.

BUTCH

Of all the fuckin' things she coulda forgot, she forgets my father's watch. I specifically reminded her not to forget it. 'Bedside table – on the kangaroo.' I said the words: 'Don't forget my father's watch.'

EXT. CITY STREET – DAY

The little Honda races toward its destination as fast as its little engine will take it.

*[INT. HONDA (MOVING) – DAY

Butch continues:

> BUTCH
> What the fuck am I doin'? Have I taken one too many hits to the head? That's gotta be it. Brain damage is the only excuse for this dumb a move. Stop the car, Butch.
>> (*he keeps on driving*)
> Stop the car, Butch.
>> (*he pays no attention to himself*)
> Butch, I'm talkin' to you. Put-your-foot-on-the-brake!

Butch's foot slams down hard on the brake.

EXT. CITY STREET – DAY

The little Honda skids to a stop in the middle of the street. Butch hops out of the car like it was on fire.

Butch begins pacing back and forth, talking to himself, oblivious to passersby and traffic.

> BUTCH
> I ain't gonna do this. This is a punchy move and I ain't punchy! Daddy would totally fuckin' understand. If he was here right now, he'd say, 'Butch, git a grip. It's a fuckin' watch, man. You lose one, ya get another. This is your life you're fuckin' around with, which you shouldn't be doin', 'cause you only got one.'

Butch continues to pace, but now he's silent. Then . . .

> This is my war. You see, Butch, what you're forgettin' is this watch isn't just a device that enables you to keep track of time. This watch is a symbol. It's a symbol of how your father, and his father before him, and his father before him, distinguished themselves in war. And when I took Marsellus Wallace's money, I started a war. This is my World War Two. That apartment in North Hollywood, that's my Wake Island. In fact, if you look at it that way, it's almost kismet that Fabienne left it behind. And

---

* Cut from completed film.

using that perspective, going back for it isn't stupid. It may be dangerous, but it's not stupid. Because there are certain things in this world that are worth going back for.

That's it, Butch has talked himself into it again. He hops in the car, starts it up and takes off.]

CUT TO:

A parking-meter-red flag rises up, then out, leaving the arrow pointing at one hour.

EXT. RESIDENTIAL STREET CORNER – DAY

Butch isn't completely reckless. He has parked his car a couple of blocks from his apartment to check things out before he goes boppin' through the front door.

EXT. ALLEY – DAY

Butch walks down the alley until he gets to another street, then he discreetly glances out.

EXT. STREET – BUTCH'S APARTMENT – DAY

Everything seems normal. More or less the right number of cars on the street. None of the parked cars appear out of place. None of them have a couple of goons sitting inside. Basically, it looks like normal morning activity in front of Butch's home.

Butch peers around a wall, taking in the vital information.

> **[BUTCH
> (to himself)*
> Everything looks hunky-dory. Looks can be deceiving, but this time I don't think they are. Why waste the manpower to stake out my place. I'd have to be a fuckin' idiot to come back here. That's how you're gonna beat 'em Butch, they keep underestimating you.]

* Cut from completed film.

Butch walks out of the alley and is ready for anything. He crosses the street and enters his apartment courtyard.

Across the street from Butch's building, on the corner, is a combination donut shop and Japanese restaurant. A big sign sticks up in the air, with the name 'Teriyaki Donut' and a graphic of a donut sticking out of a bowl of rice.

EXT. BUTCH'S APARTMENT COURTYARD – DAY

Butch is in the courtyard of his North Hollywood apartment building. Once again, everything appears normal – the laundry room, the pool, his apartment door – nothing appears disturbed.

Butch climbs the stairs leading to his apartment, number 12. He steps outside the door and listens inside. Nothing.

Butch slowly inserts the key into the door, quietly opening it.

INT. BUTCH'S APARTMENT – DAY

His apartment hasn't been touched.

He cautiously steps inside, shuts the door and takes a quick look around. Obviously, no one is there.

Butch walks into his modest kitchen, and opens the refrigerator. He takes out a carton of milk and drinks from it.

With carton in hand, Butch surveys the apartment. Then he goes to the bedroom.

His bedroom is like the rest of the apartment – neat, clean and anonymous. The only things personal in his room are a few boxing trophies, an Olympic silver medal, a framed issue of 'Ring Magazine' with Butch on the cover and a poster of Jerry Quarry and one of George Chuvalo.

Sure enough, there's the watch just like he said it was: on the bedside table, hanging on his little kangaroo statue.

He puts the milk down on the table, takes the watch, checks the time and puts it on. Smiling, Butch grabs the milk and exits the bedroom.

He walks through the apartment and back into the kitchen. He opens a cupboard and takes out a box of Pop Tarts. Putting down the milk, he opens the box, takes out two Pop Tarts and puts them in the toaster.

Butch glances to his right, his eyes fall on something.

What he sees is a small compact Czech M61 submachine gun with a huge silencer on it, lying on his kitchen counter.

BUTCH
(softly)

Holy shit.

He picks up the intimidating peace of weaponry and examines it.

Then . . . a toilet flushes.

Butch looks up to the bathroom door, which is parallel to the kitchen. There is someone behind it.

Like a rabbit caught in a radish patch, Butch freezes, not knowing what to do.

The bathroom door opens and Vincent Vega steps out of the bathroom, tightening his belt. In his hand is the book Modesty Blaise *by Peter O'Donnell.*

Vincent and Butch lock eyes.

Vincent freezes.

Butch doesn't move, except to point the M61 in Vincent's direction.

Neither man opens his mouth.

Then . . . the toaster loudly kicks up the Pop Tarts.

That's all the situation needed.

Butch's finger hits the trigger.

Muffled fire shoots out of the end of the gun.

Vincent is seemingly wracked with twenty bullets simultaneously – lifting him off his feet, propelling him through the air and crashing through the glass shower door at the end of the bathroom.

By the time Butch removes his finger from the trigger, Vincent is annihilated.

Butch stands frozen, amazed at what just happened. His look goes from the grease spot in the bathroom that was once Vincent, down to the powerful piece of artillery in his grip.

With the respect it deserves, Butch carefully places the M61 back on the kitchen counter.

Then he exits the apartment, quickly.

EXT. APARTMENT COURTYARD – DAY

Butch, not running, but walking very rapidly, crosses the courtyard . . .

. . . comes out of the apartment building, crosses the street . . .

. . . goes through the alley . . .

. . . and into his car in one steadicam shot.

EXT. HONDA – DAY

Butch cranks the car into gear and drives away. The big wide smile of a survivor breaks across his face.

EXT. APARTMENT BUILDING STREET – DAY

The Honda turns down the alley and slowly cruises by his apartment building.

INT. HONDA – DAY

Butch looks out the window at his former home.

> BUTCH
> That's how you're gonna beat 'em, Butch. They keep underestimatin' ya.

This makes the boxer laugh out loud. As he laughs, he flips a tape in the cassette player. When the music starts, he sings along with it.

He drives by the apartment, but is stopped at the light on the corner across from Teriyaki Donut.

Butch is still chuckling, singing along with the song, as we see:

THROUGH THE WINDSHIELD

the big man himself, Marsellus Wallace, exit Teriyaki Donut, carrying a box of a dozen donuts and two large styrofoam cups of coffee. He steps off the curb, crossing the street in front of Butch's car. This is the first time we see Marsellus clearly.

Laughing boy stops when he sees the big man directly in front of him.

When Marsellus is in front of Butch's car, he casually glances to his left, sees Butch, continues walking . . . then stops!

DOUBLE-TAKE: *'Am I really seeing what I'm seeing?'*

Butch doesn't wait for the big man to answer his own question. He stomps on the gas pedal.

The little Honda slams into Marsellus, sending him, the donuts and coffee hitting the pavement at thirty miles an hour.

Butch cuts into cross traffic and is broad sided by a gold Camaro Z-28, breaking all the windows in the Honda and sending it up on the sidewalk.

Butch sits dazed and confused in the crumpled mess of what at one time was Fabienne's Honda. Blood flows from his nostrils. The still-functional tape player continues to play. A pedestrian pokes his head inside.

PEDESTRIAN

Jesus, are you okay?

Butch looks at him, spaced-out.

BUTCH

I guess.

Marsellus Wallace lies sprawled out in the street. Gawkers gather around the body.

GAWKER #1
(to the others)

He's dead! He's dead!

This jerk's yelling makes Marsellus come to.

Two pedestrians help the shaken Butch out of the wreckage.

The woozy Marsellus gets to his feet.

> GAWKER #2
>
> If you need a witness in court, I'll be glad to help. That guy was a drunken maniac. He hit you and crashed into that car.

> MARSELLUS
> *(still incoherent)*
>
> Who?

> GAWKER #2
> *(pointing at Butch)*
>
> Him.

Marsellus follows the Gawker's finger and sees Butch Coolidge down the street, looking a shambles.

> MARSELLUS
>
> Well, I'll be damned.

The big man takes out a .45 Automatic and the Gawkers back away. Marsellus starts moving toward Butch.

Butch sees the fierce figure making a wobbly beeline toward him.

> BUTCH
> Sacre bleu.

Marsellus brings up his weapon and fires, but he's so hurt, shaky and dazed that his arm goes wild.

He hits a Looky-Loo Woman in the hip. She falls to the ground, screaming.

> LOOKY-LOO WOMAN
> Oh my god, I've been shot!

That's all Butch needs to see. He's outta there.

Marsellus runs after him.

The crowd looks agape.

Butch is in a mad, limping run.

The big man's hot on his ass with a cockeyed wobbly run.

Butch cuts across traffic and dashes into a business with a sign that reads: MASON-DIXON PAWNSHOP.

INT. MASON-DIXON PAWNSHOP — DAY

Maynard, a hillbilly-lookin' boy, stands behind the counter of his pawnshop when, all of a sudden, chaos in the form of Butch races into his world.

> MAYNARD
> Can I help you wit' somethin'?

> BUTCH
> Shut up!

Butch quickly takes measure of the situation, then stands next to the door.

> MAYNARD
> Now you just wait one goddamn minute –

Before Maynard can finish his threat, Marsellus charges in. He doesn't get past the doorway because Butch lands his fist in Marsellus' face.

The gangster's feet go out from under him and the big man falls flat on his back.

Outside, two police cars with their sirens blaring race by.

Butch pounces on the fallen body, punching him twice more in the face.

Butch takes the gun out of Marsellus' hand, then grabs ahold of his middle finger.

> BUTCH
>
> So you like chasing people, huh?

He breaks the finger. Marsellus lets out a pain sound. Butch then places the barrel of the .45 between his eyes, pulls back the hammer and places his open hand behind the gun to shield the splatter.

> . . . Well, guess what, big man, you caught me –

> MAYNARD
> (*off*)
> – hold it right there, godammit!

Butch and Marsellus look up at Maynard, who's brandishing a pump-action shotgun, aimed at the two men.

> BUTCH
>
> Look mister, this ain't any of your business –

> MAYNARD
> – I'm makin' it my business! Now toss that gun!

Butch does.

> . . . now you on top, stand up and come to the counter.

Butch slowly gets up and moves to the counter. As soon as he gets there, Maynard hauls off, hitting him hard in the face with the butt of the shotgun, knocking Butch down and out.

After Butch goes down, Maynard calmly lays the shotgun on the counter and moves to the telephone.

Marsellus Wallace, from his position on the floor, groggily watches the pawnshop owner dial a number. Maynard waits on the line while the other end rings. Then he picks it up.

(*into phone*)
. . . Zed? It's Maynard. The spider just caught a coupla flies.

Marsellus passes out.

FADE TO BLACK

FADE UP:

INT. PAWNSHOP BACK ROOM – DAY
TWO SHOT – BUTCH AND MARSELLUS

*are tied up in two separate chairs. In their mouths are two S&M-styled
ball gags (a belt goes around their heads and a little red ball sticks in their
mouths). Both men are unconscious. Maynard steps in with a fire
extinguisher and sprays both guys until they're wide awake and wet as
otters. The two prisoners look up at their captor.*

*Maynard stands in front of them, fire extinguisher in one hand, shotgun in
the other and Marsellus' .45 sticking in his belt.*

MAYNARD
Nobody kills anybody in my place of business except me or Zed.

A buzzer buzzes.

 . . . That's Zed.

We hear, on the other side of the curtains, Maynard let Zed inside the store.

Butch and Marsellus look around the room. The basement of the pawnshop has been converted into a dungeon. After taking in their predicament, Butch and Marsellus look at each other, all traces of hostility gone, replaced by a terror they both share at what they've gotten themselves into.

Maynard and Zed come through the curtains. Zed is an even more intense version of Maynard, if such a thing is possible. The two hillbillies are obviously brothers. Where Maynard is a vicious pitbull, Zed is deadly cobra. Zed walks in and stands in front of the two captives. He inspects them for a long time, then says:

> ZED
> (*to Maynard*)
You said you waited for me?

> MAYNARD
I did.

> ZED
Then how come they're all beat up?

> MAYNARD
They did that to each other. They was fightin' when they came in. This one was gonna shoot that one.

> ZED
> (*to Butch*)
You were gonna shoot him?

Butch makes no reply.

 Hey, is Grace gonna be okay in front of this place?

> MAYNARD
Yeah, it ain't Tuesday is it?

ZED

No, it's Thursday.

MAYNARD

Then she'll be fine

ZED

Bring out The Gimp.

MAYNARD

I think The Gimp's asleep.

ZED

Well, I guess you'll just wake 'em up then, won't you?

Maynard opens a trapdoor in the floor.

MAYNARD
(*yelling in the hole*)

Wake up!

Maynard reaches into the hole and comes back holding onto a leash. He gives it a rough yank and, from below the floor, rises The Gimp.

The Gimp is a man they keep dressed from head to toe in black leather bondage gear. There are zippers, buckles and studs here and there on the body. On his head is a black leather mask with two eyeholes and a zipper (closed) for a mouth. They keep him in a hole in the floor big enough for a large dog.

Zed takes the chair, sits it in front of the two prisoners, then lowers into it. Maynard hands The Gimp's leash to Zed, then backs away.

ZED
(*to The Gimp*)

Down!

The Gimp gets on its knees.

Maynard hangs back while Zed appraises the two men.

MAYNARD

Who's first?

ZED

I ain't fer sure yet.

Then with his little finger, Zed does a silent 'Eenie, meany, miney, moe . . .' just his mouth mouthing the words and his finger going back and forth between the two.

Butch and Marsellus are terrified.

Maynard looks back and forth at the victims.

The Gimp's eyes go from one to the other inside the mask.

Zed continues his silent singsong with his finger moving left to right, then it stops.

TWO SHOT – BUTCH AND MARSELLUS

After a beat, the camera moves to the right, zeroing in on Marsellus.

> ZED
> I guess that means you, big boy.

Zed stands up.

> Wanna do it here?

> MAYNARD
> Naw, drag big boy to Russell's old room.

> ZED
> Sounds good to me.

Zed grabs Marsellus' chair and drags him into Russell's old room. Russell, no doubt, was some other poor bastard that had the misfortune of stumbling into the Mason-Dixon pawnshop. Whatever happened to Russell is known only to Maynard and Zed because his old room, a room in the back of the back room, is empty.

As Marsellus is dragged away, he locks eyes with Butch before he disappears behind the door of Russell's old room.

> MAYNARD
> (*to The Gimp*)
> Up!

The Gimp rises. Maynard ties The Gimp's leash to a hook on the ceiling.

> . . . Keep an eye on this one.

The Gimp bows its head: 'Yes.' Maynard disappears into Russell's old room. There must be a stereo in there because suddenly The Judds, singing in harmony, fill the air.

Butch looks at The Gimp. The Gimp giggles from underneath the mask as if this were the funniest moment in the history of comedy.

From behind the door we hear country music, struggling, and:

MAYNARD
(*off*)

. . . Whoa, this boy's got a bit of fight in 'em!

We then hear Maynard and Zed beat on Marsellus.

ZED
(*off*)

You wanna fight? You wanna fight? Good, I like to fight!

Butch pauses, listens to the voices. Then, in a panic, hurriedly struggles to get free.

The Gimp is laughing wildly.

The ropes are on too tight and Butch can't break free.

The Gimp slaps his knee laughing.

In the back room we hear:

MAYNARD
(*off*)

That's it . . . that's it boy, you're goin' fine. Oooooooh, just like that . . . that's good.
(*grunting faster*)
Stay still . . . stay still goddamn ya! Zed goodamit, git over here and hold 'em!

Butch stops struggling and lifts up on his arms. Then, quite easily, the padded chair back slides up and off as if it were never connected by a bolt.

The Gimp sees this and its eyes widen.

THE GIMP

Huhng?

The Gimp flails wildly, trying to get the leash off the hook. He tries to yell, but all that comes out are excited gurgles and grunts.

Butch is out of his chair, quickly dispensing three boxer's punches to its face. The punches knock The Gimp out, making him fall to his knees. Thus hanging himself by the leash attached to the hook.

Butch removes the ball gag, then silently makes his way through the red curtains.

INT. PAWNSHOP – DAY

Butch sneaks to the door.

On the counter is a big set of keys with a large Z connected to the ring. Grabbing them, he's about to go out when he stops and listens to the hillbilly psychopaths having their way with Marsellus.

Butch decides for the life of him, he can't leave anybody in a situation like that. So he begins rooting around the pawnshop for a weapon to bash those hillbillies' heads in with.

He picks up a big destructive-looking hammer, then discards it: not destructive enough. He picks up a chainsaw, thinks about it for a moment, then puts it back. Next, a large Louisville slugger he tries on for size. But then he spots what he's been looking for:

A Samurai sword.

It hangs in its hand-carved wood sheath from a nail on the wall, next to a neon DAD'S OLD-FASHIONED ROOT BEER sign. Butch takes the sword off the wall, removing it from its sheath. It's a magnificent piece of steel. It seems to glisten in the low-wattage light of the pawnshop. Butch touches his thumb to the blade to see if the sword is just for show. Not on your life. It's as sharp as it gets. This weapon seems made to order for the Brothers Grimm downstairs. Holding the sword pointed downward, Takakura Ken-style, he disappears through the red curtains to take care of business.

INT. PAWNSHOP BACK ROOM – DAY

Butch quietly sneaks down the stairs leading to the dungeon. Sodomy and

The Judds can still be heard going strong behind the closed door that leads to Russell's old room.

INT. RUSSELL'S OLD ROOM – DAY

Butch's hand comes into frame, pushing the door open. It swings open silently, revealing the rapists, who have switched positions. Zed is now bent over Marsellus, who is bent over a wooden horse. Maynard watches. Both have their backs to Butch.

Maynard faces the camera, grinning, while Butch comes up behind him with the sword.

Miserable, violated and looking like a rag doll, Marsellus, red ball gag still in mouth, opens his watery eyes to see Butch coming up behind Maynard. His eyes widen.

> BUTCH
> Hey hillbilly.

Maynard turns and sees Butch holding the sword.

Butch screams . . . with one mighty swing, slashes Maynard across his front, moving past him, eyes and blade now locked on Zed.

Maynard stands trembling, his front sliced open, in shock.

Butch, while never taking his eyes off Zed, thrusts the sword behind him, skewering Maynard, then extracts it, pointing the blade toward Zed. Maynard collapses.

Zed disengages from Marsellus in a hurry and his eyes go from the tip of Butch's sword to Marsellus' .45 Automatic, which lies within reach.

Butch's eyes follow Zed's.

> BUTCH
> You want that gun, Zed? Pick it up.

Zed's hand inches toward the weapon.

Butch grips the sword tighter.

Zed studies Butch.

Butch looks hard at Zed.

Then a voice says:

> MARSELLUS
> (*off*)
>
> Step aside, Butch.

Butch steps aside, revealing Marsellus standing behind him, holding Maynard's pump-action shotgun.

KABOOM!!!!

Zed is blasted in the groin. Down he goes, screaming in agony.

Marsellus, looking down at his whimpering rapist, ejects the used shotgun shell.

Butch lowers the sword and hangs back. Not a word, until:

> BUTCH
>
> You okay?

> MARSELLUS
>
> Naw, man. I'm pretty fuckin' far from okay!

Long pause.

BUTCH
What now?

MARSELLUS
What now? Well, let me tell you what now. I'm gonna call a coupla pipe-hittin' niggers, who'll go to work on the homes here with a pair of pliers and a blowtorch.
(*to Zed*)
Hear me talkin', hillbilly boy?! I ain't through with you by a damn sight. I'm gonna git Medieval on your ass.

BUTCH
I meant what now, between me and you?

MARSELLUS
Oh, that 'what now?' Well, let me tell ya what now between me an' you. There is no me an' you. Not no more.

BUTCH
So we're cool?

MARSELLUS
Yeah man, we're cool. Two things I ask: don't tell nobody about this. This shit's between me and you and the soon-to-be-livin'-the-rest-of-his-short-ass-life-in-agonizing-pain, Mr Rapist here. It ain't nobody else's business. Two: leave town. Tonight. Right now. And when you're gone, stay gone. You've lost your Los Angeles privileges. Deal?

BUTCH
Deal.

The two men shake hands, then hug one another.

MARSELLUS
Go on now, get your ass outta here.

Butch leaves Russell's old room through the red curtains. Marsellus walks over to a phone, dialing a number.

*[MARSELLUS
(*into the phone*)
Hello Mr Wolf, it's Marsellus. Gotta bit of a situation.]
* Cut from completed film.

EXT.MASON-DIXON PAWNSHOP – DAY

Butch, still shaking in his boots, exits the pawnshop. He looks ahead and sees, parked in front of the establishment, Zed's Big Chrome Chopper with a teardrop gas tank that has the name GRACE *on it. He climbs aboard, takes out the keys with the big Z on them and starts up the huge hog. It rumbles to life, making sounds like a rocket fighting for orbit. Butch twists the accelerator handle and speeds off.*

WE CUT BACK AND FORTH BETWEEN . . .

INT. BUTCH AND FABIENNE'S HOTEL ROOM – DAY

Fabienne stands in front of a mirror wearing a 'Frankie says, Relax' T-shirt, singing along with music coming from a boom box.

EXT. CITY STREET – CHOPPER (MOVING) – DAY

Butch drives down the street, humping a hot hog named GRACE. *He checks his father's watch. It says:* 10:30.

The song in the motel room plays over this.

EXT. MOTEL ROOM – DAY

Butch rides up on Grace. He hops off and runs inside the motel room, while we stay outside with the bike.

> FABIENNE
> (off)

Butch, I was so worried!

> BUTCH

Honey, grab your radio and your purse and let's go!

> FABIENNE
> (off)

But what about all our bags?

> BUTCH

Fuck the bags. We'll miss our train if we don't split now.

FABIENNE
(off)
Is everything well? Are we in danger?

BUTCH
We're cool. In fact, we're super-cool. But we gots ta go. I'll wait for you outside.

Butch runs out and hops back on the bike. Fabienne exits the motel room with the boom box and a large purse. When she sees Butch on the chopper, she stops dead.

FABIENNE
Where did you get this motorcycle?

BUTCH
(*he kicks-starts it*)
It's a chopper, baby, hop on.

Fabienne slowly approaches the two-wheel demon.

FABIENNE
What happened to my Honda?

BUTCH
Sorry baby, I crashed your Honda.

FABIENNE

You're hurt?

BUTCH

I might've broke my nose, no biggie. Hop on.

She doesn't move.

Butch looks at her.

Honey, we gotta hit the fuckin' road!

Fabienne starts to cry.

Butch realizes that this is not the way to get her on the bike. He turns off the engine and reaches out, taking her hand.

I'm sorry, baby-love.

FABIENNE
(*crying*)

You were gone so long, I started to think dreadful thoughts.

BUTCH

I'm sorry I worried you, sweetie. Everything's fine. Hey, how was breakfast?

FABIENNE
(*waterworks drying a little*)

It was good —

BUTCH

— did you get the blueberry pancakes?

FABIENNE

No, they didn't have blueberry pancakes. I had to get buttermilk — are you sure you're okay?

BUTCH

Baby-love, from the moment I left you, this has been without a doubt the single weirdest day of my entire life. Climb on an' I'll tell ya about it.

Fabienne does climb on. Butch starts her up.

Butch, whose motorcycle is this?

BUTCH

It's a chopper.

FABIENNE

Whose chopper is this?

BUTCH

Zed's.

FABIENNE

Who's Zed?

BUTCH

Zed's dead, baby, Zed's dead.

And with that, the two lovebirds peel away on Grace, as the song on the boom box rises.

FADE TO BLACK

TITLE CARD:

'THE BONNIE SITUATION'

TITLE DISAPPEARS.

Over black, we can hear in the distance, men talking.

JULES
(*off*)
You ever read the Bible, Brett?

BRETT
(*off*)
Yes!

JULES
(*off*)
There's a passage I got memorized, seems appropriate for this situation. Ezekiel 25:17. 'The path of the righteous man is beset

on all sides by the inequities of the selfish and the tyranny of evil
men . . .'

FADE UP:

INT. BATHROOM – DAY

*We're in the bathroom of the Hollywood apartment we were in earlier. In
fact, we're there at exactly the same time. Except this time, we're in the
bathroom with the Fourth Man. The Fourth Man is pacing around the
small room, listening hard to what's being said on the other side of the
door, tightly clutching his huge silver .357 Magnum.*

> JULES
> (*off*)

'. . . blessed is he who, in the name of charity and good will,
shepherds the weak through the valley of darkness. And I will
strike down upon thee with great vengeance and furious anger
those who attempt to poison and destroy my brothers. And you
will know I am the Lord when I lay my vengeance upon you.'

BANG! BANG! BOOM! POW! BAM BAM BAM BAM BAM!

*The Fourth Man freaks out. He throws himself against the back wall,
gun outstretched in front of him, a look of yellow fear on his face, ready to
blow in half anybody fool enough to stick their head through that door.*

Then he listens to them talk to Marvin who is cowering in a corner.

> VINCENT
> (*off*)

Friend of yours?

> JULES
> (*off*)

Yeah, Marvin-Vincent-Vincent-Marvin.

*Waiting for them isn't the smartest move. Bursting out the door and
blowing them all away while they're fuckin' around is the way to go.*

INT. APARTMENT – DAY

The bathroom door bursts open and the Fourth Man charges out, silver Magnum raised, firing six booming shots from his hand cannon.

FOURTH MAN

Die . . . die . . . die . . . die . . . !

Dolly into Fourth Man. He screams until he's dry firing. Then, a look of confusion crosses his face.

TWO SHOT – JULES AND VINCENT
standing next to each other, unharmed. Amazing as it seems, none of the Fourth Man's shots appear to have hit anybody. Jules and Vincent exchange looks like, 'Are you hit?' They're as confused as the shooter. After looking at each other, they bring their looks up to the Fourth Man.

FOURTH MAN

I don't understand –

The Fourth Man is taken out of the scenario by the two men's bullets who, unlike his, hit their marks. He drops dead.

The two men lower their guns. Jules, obviously shaken, sits down in a chair. Vincent, after a moment of respect, shrugs it off. Then heads toward Marvin in the corner.

VINCENT

Why the fuck didn't you tell us about that guy in the bathroom? Slip your mind? Forget he was in there with a goddam hand cannon?

JULES
(*to himself*)

We should be fuckin' dead right now.
(*pause*)
Did you see that gun he fired at us? It was bigger than him.

VINCENT

·357·

JULES

We should be fuckin' dead!

137

VINCENT

Yeah, we were lucky.

Jules rises, moving toward Vincent.

JULES

That shit wasn't luck. That shit was somethin' else.

Vincent prepares to leave.

VINCENT

Yeah, maybe.

JULES

That was . . . divine intervention. You know what divine intervention is?

VINCENT

Yeah, I think so. That means God came down from heaven and stopped the bullets.

JULES

Yeah, man, that's what it means. That's exactly what it means! God came down from heaven and stopped the bullets.

VINCENT

I think we should be going now.

JULES

Don't do that! Don't you fuckin' do that! Don't blow this shit off! What just happened was a fuckin' miracle!

VINCENT

Chill the fuck out, Jules, this shit happens.

JULES

Wrong, wrong, this shit doesn't just happen.

VINCENT

Do you wanna continue this theological discussion in the car, or at the jailhouse with the cops?

JULES

We should be fuckin' dead now, my friend! We just witnessed a miracle, and I want you to fuckin' acknowledge it!

VINCENT
Okay man, it was a miracle, can we leave now?

EXT. HOLLYWOOD APARTMENT BUILDING — MORNING

The Chevy Nova propels itself into traffic.

INT. NOVA (MOVING) — MORNING

Jules is behind the wheel, Vincent in the passenger seat and Marvin in the back.

VINCENT
. . . ever seen that show 'Cops?' I was watchin' it once and this cop was on it who was talkin' about this time he got into this gun fight with a guy in a hallway. He unloads on this guy and he doesn't hit nothin'. And these guys were in a hallway. It's a freak, but it happens.

JULES
If you wanna play blind man, then go walk with a shepherd. But me, my eyes are wide fuckin' open.

VINCENT
What the fuck does that mean?

JULES
That's it for me. From here on in, you can consider my ass retired.

VINCENT
Jesus Christ!

JULES
Don't blaspheme!

VINCENT
Goddammit, Jules —

JULES
— I said don't do that —

VINCENT
— you're fuckin' freakin' out!

JULES

I'm tellin' Marsellus today I'm through.

VINCENT

While you're at it, be sure to tell 'im why.

JULES

Don't worry, I will.

VINCENT

I'll bet ya ten thousand dollars, he laughs his ass off.

JULES

I don't give a damn if he does.

Vincent turns to the back seat with the .45 casually in his grip.

VINCENT

Marvin, what do you make of all this?

MARVIN

I don't even have an opinion.

VINCENT

C'mon, Marvin. You gotta have an opinion. Do you think God came down from Heaven and stopped the bullets?

Vincent's .45 goes BANG!

Marvin is hit in the upper chest, below the throat. He gurgles blood and shakes.

JULES

What the fuck's happening?

VINCENT

I just accidentally shot Marvin in the throat.

JULES

Why the fuck did you do that?

VINCENT

I didn't meant to do it. I said it was an accident.

JULES

I've seen a lot of crazy-ass shit in my time –

VINCENT

– chill out, man, it was an accident, okay? You probably hit a bump or somethin' and the gun went off.

JULES

The car didn't hit no motherfuckin' bump!

VINCENT

Look! I didn't meant to shoot this son-of-a-bitch, the gun just went off, don't ask me how! *[Now I think the humane thing to do is put him out of his misery.

JULES
(can't believe it)
You wanna shoot 'im again?

VINCENT

The guy's sufferin'. It's the right thing to do.

Marvin, suffering though he is, is listening to this debate, not believing what he's hearing.

After a pause:

JULES

This is really uncool.

Vincent turns to the back seat, places the barrel of the .45 against Marvin's forehead. Marvin's eyes are as big as saucers. He tries to talk Vince out of this, but when he opens his mouth, only gurgles come out.

Marvin, I just wanna apologize. I got nothin' to do with this shit. And I want you to know I think it's fucked up.

VINCENT

Okay, Pontius Pilate, when I count three, honk your horn. One . . . two . . .

CU *of the steering wheel.*

. . . three.

* Cut from completed film.

142

Jules presses down hard on the horn: HONK *and* BANG!

When we cut back to the two men, the car is completely covered in blood. It's all over everything, including Jules and Vincent.

> JULES

Jesus Christ Almighty!

> VINCENT
> (*to himself*)

Fuck.]

> JULES

Look at this mess! We're drivin' around on a city street in broad daylight –

> VINCENT

– I know, I know, I wasn't thinkin' about the splatter.

> JULES

Well, you better be thinkin' about it now, motherfucker! We gotta get this car off the road. Cops tend to notice shit like you're driving a car drenched in fuckin' blood.

> VINCENT

Can't we just take it to a friendly place?

> JULES

This is the Valley, Vincent. Marsellus don't got no friendly places in the Valley.

> VINCENT

Well, don't look at me, this is your town, Jules.

Jules takes out a cellular phone and starts punching digits.

. . . Who ya callin'?

> JULES

A buddy of mine in Toluca Lake.

> VINCENT

Where's Toluca Lake?

> JULES

On the other side of the hill, by Burbank Studios. If Jimmie's ass ain't home, I don't know what the fuck we're gonna do. I ain't got any other partners in 818.

(*into phone*)

Jimmie! How ya doin' man, it's Jules.

(*pause*)

Listen up man, me an' my homeboy are in some serious shit. We're in a car we gotta get off the road, pronto! I need to use your garage for a coupla hours.

(*pause*)

*[Jimmie, you know I can't get into this shit on a cellular fuckin' phone. But what I can say is my ass is out in the cold and I'm askin' you for some sanctuary 'til our people can bring us in.

(*pause*)

We'll be gone by then.

(*pause*)

– Jimmie, I'm aware of your situation. I ain't gonna fuck things up for you. I give you my word, partner, she'll never know we were there.

(*pause*)

Five minutes. Later.

He folds up the phone, turns to Vincent.

We're set. But his wife comes home from work in an hour and a half and we gotta be outta there by then.

EXT. JIMMIE'S HOUSE – MORNING

The Nova pulls into the garage of a two-bedroom suburban house.]

INT. JIMMIE'S BATHROOM – DAY

Jules is bent over a sink, washing his bloody hands, while Vincent stands behind him.

JULES

We gotta be real fuckin' delicate with this Jimmie situation. He's one remark away from kickin' our asses out the door.

* Cut from completed film.

VINCENT

If he kicks us out, whadda we do?

JULES

Well, we ain't leavin' 'til we made a coupla phone calls. But I never want it to reach that pitch. Jimmie's my friend and you don't bust in your friend's house and start tellin' 'im what's what.

Jules rises and dries his hands. Vincent takes his place at the sink.

VINCENT

Just tell 'im not to be abusive. He kinda freaked out back there when he saw Marvin.

JULES

Well, put yourself in his position. It's eight o'clock in the morning. He just woke up. He wasn't prepared for this shit. Don't forget who's doin' who a favor.

Vincent finishes, then dries his hands on a white towel.

VINCENT

If the price of that favor is I gotta take shit, he can stick his favor straight up his ass.

When Vincent is finished drying his hands, the towel is stained with red.

JULES

What the fuck did you do to his towel?

VINCENT

I was just dryin' my hands.

JULES

You're supposed to wash 'em first.

VINCENT

You watched me wash 'em.

JULES

I watched you get 'em wet.

VINCENT

I washed 'em. Blood's real hard to get off. Maybe if he had some Lava, I coulda done a better job.

JULES

I used the same soap you did and when I dried my hands, the towel didn't look like a fuckin' Maxie pad. Look, fuck it, alright. Who cares? But it's shit like this that's gonna bring this situation to a boil. If he were to come in here and see that towel like that . . . I'm tellin' you Vincent, you best be cool. 'Cause if I gotta get into it with Jimmie on account of you . . . Look, I ain't threatenin' you, I respect you an' all, but just don't put me in that position.

VINCENT

Jules, you ask me nice like that, no problem. He's your friend, you handle him.

INT. JIMMIE'S KITCHEN – MORNING

Three men are standing in Jimmie's kitchen, each with a mug of coffee. Jules, Vincent and Jimmie Dimmick, a young man in his late-twenties dressed in a bathrobe.

JULES

Goddam Jimmie, this is some serious gourmet shit. Me an' Vincent woulda been satisfied with freeze-dried Tasters Choice. You spring this gourmet fuckin' shit on us. What flavor is this?

JIMMIE

Knock it off, Julie.

JULES

What?

JIMMIE

I'm not a cob of corn, so you can stop butterin' me up. I don't need you to tell me how good my coffee is. I'm the one who buys it, I know how fuckin' good it is. When Bonnie goes shoppin', she buys shit. I buy the gourmet expensive stuff 'cause when I drink it, I wanna taste it. But what's on my mind at this moment isn't the coffee in my kitchen, it's the dead nigger in my garage.

JULES

Jimmie –

JIMMIE

– I'm talkin'. Now let me ask you a question, Jules. When you drove in here, did you notice a sign out front said, 'Dead Nigger Storage?'

Jules starts to 'Jimmie' him –

. . . answer the question. Did you see a sign out in front of my house that said, 'Dead Nigger Storage?'

JULES
(*playing along*)

Naw man, I didn't.

JIMMIE

You know why you didn't see that sign?

JULES

Why?

JIMMIE

'Cause storin' dead niggers ain't my fuckin' business!

Jules starts to 'Jimmie' him.

. . . I ain't through! Now don't you understand that if Bonnie comes home and finds a dead body in her house, I'm gonna get divorced. No marriage counselor, no trial separation – fuckin' divorced. And I don't wanna get fuckin' divorced. The last time me an' Bonnie talked about this shit was gonna be the last time me an' Bonnie talked about this shit. Now I wanna help ya out Julie, I really do. But I ain't gonna lose my wife doin' it.

JULES

Jimmie –

JIMMIE

– don't fuckin' Jimmie me, man, I can't be Jimmied. There's nothin' you can say that's gonna make me forget I love my wife. Now she's workin' the graveyard shift at the hospital. She'll be comin' home in less than an hour and a half. Make your phone calls, talk to your people, then get the fuck out of my house.

JULES

That's all we want. We don't wanna fuck up your shit. We just need to call our people to bring us in.

JIMMIE

Then I suggest you get to it. Phone's in my bedroom.

*[As Jules crosses the room, exiting:

JULES
(calling behind him)
You're a friend, Jimmie, you're a good fuckin' friend!

JIMMIE
(to himself)
Yeah, yeah, yeah, yeah, yeah. I'm a real good friend. Good friend, bad husband, soon to be ex-husband.
(looks up and sees Vincent)
Who the fuck are you?

VINCENT

I'm Vincent. And Jimmie, thanks a bunch.

The two men laugh.

JIMMIE

Don't mention it.]

INT. MARSELLUS WALLACE'S DINING ROOM — MORNING

Marsellus Wallace sits at his dining table in a big comfy robe, eating his large breakfast, while talking on the phone. Mia walks toward the table.

MARSELLUS

. . . well, say she comes home. Whaddya think she'll do?
(pause)
No fuckin' shit she'll freak. That ain't no kinda answer. You know 'er, I don't. How bad, a lot or a little?

* Cut from completed film.

INT. JIMMIE'S BEDROOM – MORNING

Jules paces around in Jimmie's bedroom on the phone.

JULES

You got to appreciate what an explosive element this Bonnie situation is. If she comes home from a hard day's work and finds a bunch of gangsters doin' a bunch of gangsta' shit in her kitchen, ain't no tellin' what she's apt to do.

*[MARSELLUS

Let us speak of the unspeakable.

JULES

Possibility exists, but unlikely.

MARSELLUS

Why possible but unlikely?

JULES

'Cause if push met shove, you know I'll take care of business. But push ain't never gonna meet shove. Because you're gonna solve this shit fer us. You're gonna take our asses outta the cold and

* Cut from completed film.

bring it inside where it's warm. 'Cause if I gotta get into it with my friend about his wife over your boy Vincent, I'm gonna have bad feelings.]

                              MARSELLUS
I've grasped that, Jules. All I'm doin' is contemplating the 'ifs'.

                              JULES
I don't wanna hear about no motherfuckin' 'ifs'. What I wanna hear from your ass is: 'You ain't got no problems, Jules. I'm on the motherfucker. Go back in there, chill them niggers out and wait for the cavalry, which should be comin' directly.'

                              MARSELLUS
You ain't got no problems, Jules. I'm on the motherfucker. Go back in there, chill them niggers out and wait for The Wolf, who should be comin' directly.

                              JULES
You sendin' The Wolf?

                              MARSELLUS
Feel better?

                              JULES
Shit Negro, that's all you had to say.

INT. HOTEL SUITE – MORNING

The camera looks through the doorway of a hotel suite into the main area. We see a crap game being played on a fancy crap table by gamblers in tuxedos and lucky ladies in fancy evening gowns. The camera pans to the right revealing: sitting on a bed, phone in hand with his back to us, the tuxedo-clad Winston Wolf aka 'The Wolf.'

We also see The Wolf has a small notepad that he jots details in.

                              THE WOLF
                          (*into phone*)
Is she the hysterical type?

                          (*pause*)
When she due?

                          (*jotting down*)

Give me the principals' names again?
                              (*jots down*)
Jules . . .

We see his book. The page has written on it:

> *1265 Riverside Drive*
> *Toluca Lake*
> *1 body (no head)*
> *Bloody shot-up car*
> *Jules (black)*

                          THE WOLF
. . . Vincent . . . Jimmie . . . Bonnie . . .

He writes:

> *Vincent (Dean Martin)*
> *Jimmie (house)*
> *Bonnie (9:30)*

. . . Expect a call around 10:30. It's about thirty minutes away. I'll
be there in ten.

He hangs up. We never see his face.

CUT TO:

TITLE CARD OVER BLACK:

     'NINE MINUTES AND THIRTY-SEVEN SECONDS LATER'

CUT TO:

EXT. JIMMIE'S STREET – MORNING

*A silver Porsche whips the corner leading to Jimmie's home, in hyper
drive. Easily doing 135 mph, the Porsche stops on a dime in front of
Jimmie's house.*

A ringed finger touches the doorbell: DING DONG.

Jimmie opens the door. We see, standing in the doorway, the tuxedo-clad man. He looks down to his notebook, then up at Jimmie.

THE WOLF
You're Jimmie, right? This is your house?

JIMMIE
Yeah.

THE WOLF
(*sticks his hand out*)
I'm Winston Wolf, I solve problems.

JIMMIE
Good, 'cause we got one.

THE WOLF
So I heard. May I come in?

JIMMIE
Please do.

[The two men walk to the dining room.

THE WOLF
I want to convey Mr Wallace's gratitude with the help you're providing on this matter. Let me assure you, Jimmie, Mr Wallace's gratitude is worth having.]

In the dining room, Jules and Vincent stand up.

You must be Jules, which would make you Vincent. Let's get down to brass tacks, gentlemen. If I was informed correctly, the clock is ticking, is that right, Jimmie?

JIMMIE
100 per cent.

THE WOLF
Your wife, Bonnie . . .
(*refers to his pad*)
. . . comes home at 9:30 in the A.M., is that correct?

* Cut from completed film.

JIMMIE

Uh-huh.

THE WOLF

I was led to believe if she comes home and finds us here, she wouldn't appreciate it none too much.

JIMMIE

She won't at that.

THE WOLF

That gives us forty minutes to get the fuck outta Dodge, which, if you do what I say when I say it, should be plenty. Now you got a corpse in a car, minus a head, in a garage. Take me to it.

INT. JIMMIE'S GARAGE – MORNING

The three men hang back as The Wolf examines the car. He studies the car in silence, opening the door, looking inside, circling it.

THE WOLF

Jimmie?

JIMMIE

Yes.

THE WOLF

Do me a favor, will ya? Thought I smelled some coffee in there. Would you make me a cup?

JIMMIE

Sure, how do you take it?

THE WOLF

Lotsa cream, lotsa sugar.

Jimmie exits. The Wolf continues his examination.

. . . About the car, is there anything I need to know? Does it stall, does it make a lot of noise, does it smoke, is there gas in it, anything?

JULES

Aside from how it looks, the car's cool.

154

THE WOLF
Positive? Don't let me out on the road and I find the brake lights don't work.

JULES
Hey man, as far as I know, the motherfucker's tiptop.

THE WOLF
Good enough, let's go back to the kitchen.

INT. KITCHEN – MORNING

Jimmie hands The Wolf a cup of coffee.

THE WOLF
Thank you, Jimmie.

He takes a sip, then nods to Jimmie indicating that the coffee is good. Pacing as he thinks, The Wolf lays out for the three men the plan of action.

. . . Okay, first thing, you two
               (*meaning Jules and Vincent*)
take the body, stick it in the trunk. Now Jimmie, this looks to be a pretty domesticated house. That would lead me to believe that in the garage or under the sink, you got a bunch of cleaners and cleansers and shit like that, am I correct?

JIMMIE
Yeah. Exactly. Under the sink.

THE WOLF
Good. What I need you two fellas to do is take those cleaning products and clean the inside of the car. And I'm talkin' fast, fast, fast. You need to go in the back seat, scoop up all those little pieces of brain and skull. Get it out of there. Wipe down the upholstery – now, when it comes to upholstery, it don't need to be spic and span, you don't need to eat off it. Give it a good once over. What you need to take care of are the really messy parts. The pools of blood that have collected, you gotta soak that shit up. But the windows are a different story. Them you really clean. Get the Windex, do a good job. Now Jimmie, we need to raid your linen

closet. I need blankets, I need comforters, I need quilts, I need
bedspreads. The thicker the better, the darker the better. No
whites, can't use 'em. We need to camouflage the interior of the
car. We're gonna line the front seat and the back seat and the
floorboards with quilts and blankets. If a cop stops us and starts
stickin' his big snout in the car, the subterfuge won't last. But at a
glance, the car will appear to be normal. Jimmie – lead the way,
boys – get to work.

*The Wolf and Jimmie turn, heading for the bedroom, leaving Vincent
and Jules standing in the kitchen.*

> VINCENT
> (*calling after him*)

A 'please' would be nice.

The Wolf stops and turns around.

> THE WOLF

Come again?

> VINCENT

I said a 'please' would be nice.

The Wolf takes a step toward him.

> THE WOLF

Get it straight, Buster. I'm not here to say 'please'. I'm here to tell
you what to do. And if self-preservation is an instinct you possess,
you better fuckin' do it and do it quick. I'm here to help. If my
help's not appreciated, lotsa luck gentlemen.

> JULES

It ain't that way, Mr Wolf. Your help is definitely appreciated.

> VINCENT

I don't mean any disrespect. I just don't like people barkin' orders
at me.

> THE WOLF

If I'm curt with you, it's because time is a factor. I think fast, I
talk fast and I need you guys to act fast if you want to get out of
this. So pretty please, with sugar on top, clean the fuckin' car.

Jimmie's gathering all the bedspreads, quilts and linen he has. The Wolf is on the phone.

> THE WOLF
> (*into phone*)

It's a 1974 Chevy Nova.

> (*pause*)

White.

> (*pause*)

Nothin', except for the mess inside.

> (*pause*)

About twenty minutes.

> (*pause*)

Nobody who'll be missed.

> (*pause*)

You're a good man, Joe. See ya soon.

> (*he looks to Jimmie*)

How we comin', Jimmie?

Jimmie comes over with a handful of linen.

> JIMMIE

Oh, pretty good. I got it all here. But, Mr Wolf, you gotta understand somethin' –

> THE WOLF

– Winston, Jimmie – please, Winston.

> JIMMIE

Okay, you gotta understand something, Winston. I want to help you guys out and all, but that's my best linen. It was a wedding present from my Uncle Conrad and Aunt Ginny, and they ain't with us anymore –

> THE WOLF

– let me ask you a question, if you don't mind?

> JIMMIE

Sure.

THE WOLF

Were your Uncle Conrad and Aunt Ginny millionaires?

JIMMIE

No.

THE WOLF

Well, your Uncle Marsellus is. And I'm positive if Uncle Conrad
and Aunt Ginny were millionaires, they would've furnished you
with a whole bedroom set, which your Uncle Marsellus is more
than happy to do.
                    (takes out a roll of bills)
I like oak myself, that's what's in my bedroom. How 'bout you
Jimmie, you an oak man?

JIMMIE

Oak's nice.

INT. GARAGE – MORNING

*Both Jules and Vincent are inside the car cleaning it up. Vincent is in
the front seat washing windows, while Jules is in the back seat, picking
up little pieces of skull and gobs of brain. Both are twice as bloody as
they were before.*

JULES

I will never forgive your ass for this shit. This is some fucked-up
repugnant shit!

VINCENT

Jules, did you ever hear the philosophy that once a man admits
he's wrong, he's immediately forgiven for all wrongdoings?

JULES

Man, get outta my face with that shit! The motherfucker who
said that never had to pick up itty-bitty pieces of skull with his
fingers on account of your dumb ass.

VINCENT

I got a threshold, Jules. I got a threshold for the abuse I'll take.
And you're crossin' it. I'm a race car and you got me in the red.
Redline 7000, that's where you are. Just know, it's fuckin'

dangerous to be drivin' a race car when it's in the red. It could blow.

JULES

You're gettin' ready to blow? I'm a mushroom-cloud-layin' motherfucker! Every time my fingers touch brain I'm 'Superfly TNT,' I'm the *Guns of Navarone*. I'm what Jimmie Walker usta talk about. In fact, what the fuck am I doin' in the back? You're the motherfucker should be on brain detail. We're tradin'. I'm washin' windows and you're pickin' up this nigger's skull.

INT. CHEVY NOVA — MORNING

The interior of the car has been cleaned and lined with bedspreads and quilts. Believe it or not, what looked like a portable slaughterhouse can actually pass for a nondescript vehicle.

The Wolf circles the car, examining it.

Jules and Vincent stand aside, their clothes are literally a bloody mess, but they do have a sense of pride in what a good job they've done.

THE WOLF

Fine job, gentlemen. We may get out of this yet.

JIMMIE

I can't believe that's the same car.

THE WOLF

Well, let's not start suckin' each other's dicks quite yet. Phase one is complete, clean the car, which moves us right along to phase two, clean you two.

EXT. JIMMIE'S BACKYARD — MORNING

Jules and Vincent stand side by side in their black suits, covered in blood, in Jimmie's backyard. Jimmie holds a plastic Hefty trash bag, while The Wolf holds a garden hose with one of those gun nozzles attached.

THE WOLF

Strip.

VINCENT

All the way?

THE WOLF

To your bare ass.

As they follow directions, The Wolf enjoys a smoke.

. . . Quickly, gentlemen, we got about fifteen minutes before Jimmie's better half comes pulling into the driveway.

JULES

This morning air is some chilly shit.

VINCENT

Are you sure this is absolutely necessary?

THE WOLF

You know what you two look like?

VINCENT

What?

THE WOLF

Like a coupla guys who just blew off somebody's head. Yes, strippin' off those bloody rags is absolutely necessary. Toss the clothes in Jim's garbage bag.

JULES

Now Jimmie, don't do nothin' stupid like puttin' that out in front of your house for Elmo the garbage man to take away.

THE WOLF

Don't worry, we're takin' it with us. Jim, the soap.

He hands the now-naked men a bar of soap.

. . . Okay, gentlemen, you've both been to County before, I'm sure. Here it comes.

He hits the trigger, water shoots out, smacking both men.

JULES

Goddamn, that water's fuckin' cold!

Better you than me, gentlemen.

The two men, trembling, scrub themselves.

. . . Don't be afraid of the soap, spread it around.

The Wolf stops the hose, tossing it on the ground.

. . . Towel 'em.

Jimmie tosses them each a towel, which they rub furiously across their bodies.

. . . You're dry enough. Give 'em their clothes.

*[JIMMIE
Okay fellas, in the one-size-fits-all category, we got swim trunks, one red – one white. And two extra-large T-shirts. A UC Santa Cruz shirt and an 'I'm with Stupid' shirt.

JULES
I get the 'I'm with Stupid' shirt.]

FADE UP ON:

JULES AND VINCENT

In their T-shirts and swim trunks. They look a million miles away from the black-suited, bad-asses we first met.

THE WOLF
Perfect. Perfect. We couldn't've planned this better. You guys look like . . . what do they look like, Jimmie?

JIMMIE
Dorks. They look like a couple of dorks.

The Wolf and Jimmie laugh.

JULES
Ha ha ha. They're your clothes, motherfucker.

* Cut from completed film.

*[JIMMIE
I guess you just gotta know how to wear them.

JULES
Yeah, well, our asses ain't the expert on wearin' dorky shit that yours is.]

THE WOLF
C'mon, gentlemen, we're laughin' and jokin' our way into prison. Don't make me beg.

*[*They start walking through the house to the garage.*

JIMMIE
Wait a minute, before you guys split, I wanna get a picture of this.

JULES
Jimmie, have you forgotten about your wife comin' home?

JIMMIE
It won't take a second.

VINCENT
I don't like this photograph shit.

JIMMIE
Sorry – my house, my rules.]

INT. JIMMIE'S GARAGE – MORNING

The garbage bag is tossed in the car trunk on top of Marvin. The Wolf slams it closed.

THE WOLF
Gentlemen, let's get our rules of the road straight. We're going to a place called Monster Joe's Truck and Tow. Monster Joe and his daughter Raquel are sympathetic to our dilemma. The place is North Hollywood, so a few twist and turns aside, we'll be goin' up Hollywood Way. Now I'll drive the tainted car. Jules, you ride with me. Vincent, you follow in my Porsche. Now if we cross the path of any John Q. Laws, nobody does a fuckin' thing 'till I do something.

---

* Cut from completed film.

(*to Jules*)
What did I say?

JULES

Don't do shit unless –

THE WOLF

– unless what?

JULES

Unless you do it first.

THE WOLF

Spoken like a true prodigy.
(*to Vincent*)
How 'bout you, Lash Larue? Can you keep your spurs from jingling and jangling?

VINCENT

I'm cool, Mr Wolf. My gun just went off, I dunno how.

THE WOLF

Fair enough.
(*he throws Vince his car keys*)
I drive real fuckin' fast, so keep up. If I get my car back any different than I gave it, Monster Joe's gonna be disposing of two bodies.

*[JULES

Why do you drive fast?

THE WOLF

Because it's a lot of fun.

Jules and Vincent laugh.

. . . Let's move.

Jimmie comes through the door, camera in hand.

JIMMIE

Wait a minute, I wanna take a picture.

* Cut from completed film.

We ain't got time, man.

JIMMIE

We got time for one picture. You and Vincent get together.

Jules and Vincent stand next to each other.

. . . Okay, you guys, put your arms around each other.

The two men look at each other and, after a long beat, a smile breaks out. They put their arms around each other.

. . . Okay Winston, get in there.

THE WOLF

I ain't no model.

JIMMIE

After what a cool guy I've been, I can't believe you do me like this. It's the only thing I asked.

JULES AND VINCENT

C'mon, Mr Wolf . . .

THE WOLF

Okay, one photo and we go.

Slow dolly toward a lone camera.

JIMMIE
(*off*)

Everybody say Pepsi.

JULES
(*off*)

I ain't fuckin' sayin' Pepsi.

JIMMIE
(*off*)

Smile, Winston.

THE WOLF

I don't smile in pictures.

The camera goes off, flashing the screen white.

THE PHOTO FADES UP OVER WHITE:

It's Jules and Vincent, their arms around each other, next to Jimmie, whose arm is around The Wolf. Everyone is smiling except you-know-who.

INT. MONSTER JOE'S TRUCK AND TOW — MORNING

Winston is counting out three thousand dollars to an older man in a dirty T-shirt, Monster Joe. We're in Joe's office, which looks like the office of every tow yard on the planet. A filthy, disarrayed mess.

> MONSTER JOE
> I've said it before, I'll say it again, your business is always welcome.

> WINSTON
> I would think by now I've earned the equivalent of Frequent Flyer miles.

> MONSTER JOE
> I'll tell ya what, if you ever need it, I'll dispose of a body part for free.

> WINSTON
> How 'bout an upgrade, you dispose a whole body for the price of a body part.

The two men laugh.

> MONSTER JOE
> That one I need to speak with my accountant on.

> WINSTON
> Where's that reprobate daughter of yours?

> MONSTER JOE
> Out in the yard, up to no good.

EXT. MONSTER JOE'S TRUCK AND TOW — MORNING

Winston steps outside and is joined by Monster Joe's daughter, Raquel. They walk in step across the yard with their arms around each other's waists.

RAQUEL
Hello, Boyfriend!

WINSTON
Hello, Girlfriend. I swear, heartbreaker, Joe should change the name of this place to Beauty and the Beast Truck and Tow.

RAQUEL
You're prejudiced because you love me.

WINSTON
Guilty.

RAQUEL
Now business is done, it's time for pleasure.

WINSTON
The time it is, is time for bed.

RAQUEL
Contre senior Lobo.

WINSTON
Do you have a different idea?

RAQUEL
Most definitely.

WINSTON
What do you think?

RAQUEL
I think you're taking me out to breakfast.

WINSTON
Well, you thought wrong.

RAQUEL
That's not fair! I never get to see you.

WINSTON
Raquel, I been up all night. I need sleep. You understand the concept of sleep?

RAQUEL
Yes, sleep is what you do after you've taken me to breakfast. Just

get used to the idea, indulging me is the price of doing business at Monster Joe's Truck and Tow.

WINSTON

Raquel –

RAQUEL

I haven't seen you in a long time. I miss you, we're going to breakfast. So it is written, so shall it be done.

They exit the tow yard.] Jules and Vincent wait by Winston's Porsche.

JULES

We cool?

WINSTON

Like it never happened.

Jules and Vincent bump fists.

*[JULES

I apologize for bein' in your shit like I was.

VINCENT

You had every right, I fucked up.

RAQUEL
(*to Winston*)

Are they having a moment?]

WINSTON

Boys, this is Raquel. Someday, all this will be hers.

RAQUEL
(*to the boys*)

Hi. You know, if they ever do *I Spy: The Motion Picture*, you guys, I'd be great. What's with the outfits. You guys going to a volleyball game?

Winston laughs, the boys groan.

WINSTON

I'm takin' m'lady out to breakfast. Maybe I can drop you two off. Where do you live?

* Cut from completed film.

VINCENT

Redondo Beach.

JULES

Inglewood.

Winston grabs Jules' wrist and pantomimes like he's in a Dead Zone trance.

WINSTON
(*painfully*)
It's your future: I see . . . a cab ride.
(*dropping the act*)
Sorry guys, move out of the sticks.
(*to Raquel*)
Say goodbye, Raquel.

RAQUEL

Goodbye, Raquel.

WINSTON

I'll see you two around, and stay outta trouble, you crazy kids.

Winston turns to leave.

JULES

Mr Wolf.

He turns around.

. . . It was a pleasure watchin' you work.

The Wolf smiles.

WINSTON

Call me Winston.

He turns and banters with Raquel as they get in the Porsche.

. . . You hear that, young lady? Respect. You could learn a lot from those two fine specimens. Respect for one's elders shows character.

RAQUEL

I have character.

WINSTON

Just because you are a character doesn't mean you have character.

RAQUEL

Oh you're so funny, oh you're so funny.

The Porsche shoots off down the road.

The two men are left alone to look at each other.

JULES

Wanna share a cab?

VINCENT

You know I could go for some breakfast. Want to have breakfast with me?

JULES

Sure.

INT. COFFEE SHOP – MORNING

Jules and Vincent sit at a booth. In front of Vincent is a big stack of pancakes and sausages, which he eats with gusto.

Jules, on the other hand, just has a cup of coffee and a muffin. He seems far away in thought. The Waitress pours a refill for both men.

VINCENT

Thanks a bunch.
                    (*to Jules, who's nursing his coffee*)
Want a sausage?

JULES

Naw, I don't eat pork.

VINCENT

Are you Jewish?

JULES

I ain't Jewish, man, I just don't dig on swine.

VINCENT

Why not?

JULES

They're filthy animals. I don't eat filthy animals.

VINCENT

Sausages taste good. Pork chops taste good.

JULES

A sewer rat may taste like pumpkin pie. I'll never know 'cause
even if it did, I wouldn't eat the filthy motherfucker. Pigs sleep
and root in shit. That's a filthy animal. I don't wanna eat nothin'
that ain't got enough sense to disregard its own feces.

VINCENT

How about dogs? Dogs eat their own feces.

JULES

I don't eat dog either.

VINCENT

Yes, but do you consider a dog to be a filthy animal?

JULES

I wouldn't go so far as to call a dog filthy, but they're definitely
dirty. But a dog's got personality. And personality goes a long
way.

VINCENT

So by that rationale, if a pig had a better personality, he'd cease to be a filthy animal?

JULES

We'd have to be talkin' 'bout one motherfuckin' charmin' pig. It'd have to be the Cary Grant of pigs.

The two men laugh.

VINCENT

Good for you. Lighten up a little. You been sittin' there all quiet.

JULES

I just been sittin' here thinkin'.

VINCENT
(*mouthful of food*)

About what?

JULES

The miracle we witnessed.

VINCENT

The miracle *you* witnessed. *I* witnessed a freak occurrence.

JULES

Do you know what a miracle is?

VINCENT

An act of God.

JULES

What's an act of God?

VINCENT

I guess it's when God makes the impossible possible. And I'm sorry, Jules, but I don't think what happened this morning qualifies.

JULES

Don't you see, Vince, that shit don't matter. You're judging this thing the wrong way. It's not about *what*. It could be God stopped the bullets, he changed Coke into Pepsi, he found my fuckin' car keys. You don't judge shit like this based on merit. Whether or not what we experienced was an according-to-Hoyle miracle is insignificant. What is significant is I felt God's touch. God got involved.

                    VINCENT
But why?

                    JULES
That's what's fuckin' wit' me! I don't know why. But I can't go back to sleep.

                    VINCENT
So you're serious, you're really gonna quit?

                    JULES
The life, most definitely.

Vincent takes a bite of food. Jules takes a sip of coffee. In the background, we see a Patron call the Waitress.

                    PATRON
Garçon! Coffee!

We recognize the patron to be Pumpkin from the first scene of Pumpkin and Honey Bunny.

                    VINCENT
So if you're quitting the life, what'll you do?

                    JULES
That's what I've been sitting here contemplating. First, I'm gonna deliver this case to Marsellus. Then, basically, I'm gonna walk the earth.

                    VINCENT
What do you mean, walk the earth?

                    JULES
You know, like Caine in 'Kung Fu'. Just walk from town to town, meet people, get in adventures.

                    VINCENT
How long do you intend to walk the earth?

JULES

Until God puts me where he wants me to be.

VINCENT

What if he never does?

JULES

If it takes forever, I'll wait forever.

VINCENT

So you decided to be a bum?

JULES

I'll just be Jules, Vincent – no more, no less.

VINCENT

No Jules, you're gonna be like those pieces of shit out there who beg for change. They walk around like a bunch of fuckin' zombies, they sleep in garbage bins, they eat what I throw away, and dogs piss on 'em. They got a word for 'em, they're called *bums*. And without a job, residence or legal tender, that's what you're gonna be – a fuckin' bum!

JULES

Look my friend, this is just where me and you differ –

VINCENT

– what happened was peculiar – no doubt about it – but it wasn't water into wine.

JULES

All shapes and sizes, Vince.

VINCENT

Stop fuckin' talkin' like that!

JULES

If you find my answers frightening, Vincent, you should cease askin' scary questions.

*[VINCENT

When did you make this decision – while you were sitting there eatin' your muffin?

* Cut from completed film.

JULES

Yeah. I was just sitting here drinking my coffee, eating my muffin, playin' the incident in my head, when I had what alcoholics refer to as a 'moment of clarity'.]

VINCENT

I gotta take a shit. To be continued.

Vincent exits for the restroom.

Jules, alone, takes a mouthful of muffin, then . . . Pumpkin and Honey Bunny rise with guns raised.

PUMPKIN

Everybody be cool, this is a robbery!

HONEY BUNNY

Any of you fuckin' pricks move and I'll execute every one of you motherfuckers! Got that?!

Jules looks up, not believing what he's seeing. Under the table, Jules' hand goes to his .45 Automatic. He pulls it out, cocking it.

PUMPKIN

Customers stay seated, waitresses on the floor.

HONEY BUNNY

Now means fuckin' *now*! Do it or die, do it or fucking die!

Like lightning, Pumpkin moves over to the kitchen, while Honey Bunny screams out threats to the Patrons, keeping them terrified.

PUMPKIN

You Mexicans in the kitchen, get out here! *Asta luego!*

Three Cooks and two Busboys come out of the kitchen.

. . . On the floor or I'll cook your ass, *comprende?*

They comprende. *The portly Manager speaks up.*

MANAGER

I'm the manager here, there's no problem, no problem at all –

Pumpkin heads his way.

PUMPKIN

You're gonna give me a problem?

He reaches him and sticks the barrel of his gun hard in the Manager's neck.

. . . What? You said you're gonna give me a problem?

MANAGER

No, I'm not. I'm not gonna give you any problems!

PUMPKIN

I don't know, Honey Bunny. He looks like the hero type to me!

HONEY BUNNY

Don't take any chances. Execute him!

The Patrons scream. Jules watches all this silently, his hand tightly gripping the .45 Automatic under the table.

MANAGER

Please don't! I'm not a hero. I'm just a coffee-shop manager. Take anything you want.

PUMPKIN

Tell everybody to cooperate and it'll be all over.

MANAGER

Everybody just be calm and cooperate with them and this will be all over soon!

PUMPKIN

Well done, now get your fuckin' ass on the ground.

INT. COFFEE SHOP BATHROOM – MORNING

Vincent, on the toilet, oblivious to the pandemonium outside, reads his Modesty Blaise book.

INT. COFFEE SHOP – MORNING

Cash register drawer opens. Pumpkin stuffs the money from the till in his pocket. Then walks from behind the counter with a trash bag in his hand.

PUMPKIN

Okay people, I'm going to go 'round and collect your wallets.
Don't talk, just toss 'em in the bag. We clear?

Pumpkin goes around collecting wallets. Jules sits with his .45 ready to spit under the table.

Pumpkin sees Jules sitting in his booth, holding his wallet, briefcase next to him. Pumpkin crosses to him, his tone more respectful, his manner more on guard.

. . . In the bag.

Jules drops his wallet in the bag. Using his gun as a pointer, Pumpkin points to the briefcase.

. . . What's in that?

JULES

My boss's dirty laundry.

PUMPKIN

Your boss makes you do his laundry?

JULES

When he wants it clean.

PUMPKIN

Sounds like a shit job.

JULES

Funny, I've been thinkin' the same thing.

PUMPKIN

Open it up.

Jules' free hand lays palm flat on the briefcase.

JULES

'Fraid I can't do that.

Pumpkin is definitely surprised by his answer. He aims the gun right in the middle of Jules' face and pulls back the hammer.

PUMPKIN

I didn't hear you.

JULES

Yes, you did.

This exchange has been kind of quiet, not everybody heard it, but Honey Bunny senses something's wrong.

HONEY BUNNY

What's goin' on?

PUMPKIN

Looks like we got a vigilante in our midst.

HONEY BUNNY

Shoot 'em in the face!

JULES

I don't mean to shatter your ego, but this ain't the first time I've had a gun pointed at me.

PUMPKIN

You don't open up that case, it's gonna be the last.

MANAGER
(*on the ground*)

Quit causing problems, you'll get us all killed! Give 'em what you got and get 'em out of here.

JULES

Keep your fuckin' mouth closed, fat man, this ain't any of your goddamn business!

PUMPKIN

I'm countin' to three, and if your hand ain't off that case, I'm gonna unload right in your fuckin' face. Clear? One . . .

Jules closes his eyes.

. . . two . . .

*[Jules shoots Pumpkin twice, up through the table, sending him to the floor. While still in the booth, he swings around to Honey Bunny, who has aimed at Jules, but slowed down by the shock of Pumpkin getting shot. He fires three times.

* Cut from completed film.

Honey Bunny takes all three hits in the chest. As she falls screaming, she fires wildly, hitting a Surfer patron.

SURFER

She shot me! I'm dying! Sally! Sally!

Jules now brings the gun down to Pumpkin's face. Pumpkin lies shot on the floor at Jules' feet. Pumpkin looks up at the big gun.

JULES

Wrong guy, Ringo.

Jules fires straight at the camera, blinding us with his flash.

Jules' eyes, still closed, suddenly open.]

Pumpkin still stands, holding the gun on him.

PUMPKIN

. . . three.

JULES

You win.

Jules raises his hand off the briefcase.

. . . It's all yours, Ringo.

PUMPKIN

Open it.

Jules flips the locks and opens the case, revealing it to Pumpkin but not us. The same light shines from the case. Pumpkin's expression goes to amazement. Honey Bunny, across the room, can't see shit.

HONEY BUNNY

What is it? What is it?

PUMPKIN
(softly)

Is that what I think it is?

Jules nods his head: 'Yes'.

It's beautiful.

Jules nods his head: 'Yes'.

Goddammit, what is it?

Jules slams the case closed, then sits back, as if offering the case to Pumpkin. Pumpkin, one big smile, bends over to pick up the case.

Like a rattlesnake, Jules' free hand grabs the wrist of Pumpkin's gun hand, slamming it on the table. His other hand comes from under the table and sticks the barrel of his .45 hard under Pumpkin's chin.

Honey Bunny freaks out, waving her gun in Jules' direction.

. . . Let him go! Let him go! I'll blow your fuckin' head off! I'll kill ya! I'll kill ya! You're gonna die, you're gonna fuckin' die bad!

JULES
(*to Pumpkin*)
Tell that bitch to be cool! Say, bitch be cool! Say, bitch be cool!

PUMPKIN

Be cool, honey!

HONEY BUNNY

Let him go!

JULES
(*softly*)

Tell her it's gonna be okay.

PUMPKIN

It's gonna be okay.

JULES

Promise her.

PUMPKIN

I promise.

JULES

Tell her to chill.

PUMPKIN

Just chill out.

JULES

What's her name?

PUMPKIN

Yolanda.

Whenever Jules talks to Yolanda, he never looks at her, only at Pumpkin.

JULES
(*to Yolanda*)

So, we cool, Yolanda? We ain't gonna do anything stupid, are we?

YOLANDA
(*crying*)

Don't hurt him.

JULES

Nobody's gonna hurt anybody. We're gonna be like three Fonzies. And what's Fonzie like?

No answer.

. . . C'mon Yolanda, what's Fonzie like?

YOLANDA
(*through tears, unsure*)

He's cool?

JULES

Correct-amundo. And that's what we're gonna be, we're gonna be cool.

(*to Pumpkin*)

Now Ringo, I'm gonna count to three and I want you to let go your gun and lay your palms flat on the table. But when you do it, do it cool. Ready?

Pumpkin looks at him.

. . . One . . . two . . . three.

Pumpkin lets go of his gun and places both hands on the table. Yolanda can't stand it anymore.

YOLANDA

Okay, now let him go!

JULES

Yolanda, I thought you were gonna be cool. When you yell at me, it makes me nervous. When I get nervous, I get scared. And when motherfuckers get scared, that's when motherfuckers get accidentally shot.

YOLANDA
(*more conversational*)

Just know: you hurt him, you die.

JULES

That seems to be the situation. Now I don't want that and Ringo here don't want that. So let's see what we can do.

(*to Ringo*)

Now this is the situation. Normally both of your asses would be dead as fuckin' fried chicken. But you happened to pull this shit while I'm in a transitional period. I don't wanna kill ya, I want to help ya. But I'm afraid I can't give you the case. It don't belong to me. Besides, I went through too much shit this morning on account of this case to just hand it over to your ass.

VINCENT
(off)
What the fuck's goin' on here?

Yolanda whips her gun toward the stranger.

Vincent, by the bathroom, has his gun out, dead-aimed at Yolanda.

JULES
It's cool, Vincent! It's cool! Don't do a goddamn thing. Yolanda, it's cool baby, nothin's changed. We're still just talkin'.
(*to Pumpkin*)
Tell her we're still cool.

PUMPKIN
It's cool, Honey Bunny, we're still cool.

VINCENT
(*gun raised*)
What the hell's goin' on, Jules?

JULES
Nothin' I can't handle. I want you to just hang back and don't do shit unless it's absolutely necessary.

VINCENT
Check.

JULES
Yolanda, how we doin', baby?

YOLANDA
I gotta go pee! I want to go home.

JULES
Just hang in there, baby, you're doin' great. Ringo's proud of you and so am I. It's almost over.
(*to Pumpkin*)
Now I want you to go in that bag and find my wallet.

PUMPKIN
Which one is it?

JULES
It's the one that says 'Bad Motherfucker' on it.

Pumpkin looks in the bag and – sure enough – there's a wallet with 'Bad Motherfucker' embroidered on it.

. . . That's my bad motherfucker. Now open it up and take out the cash. How much is there?

PUMPKIN

About fifteen hundred dollars.

JULES

Put it in your pocket, it's yours. Now with the rest of them wallets and the register, that makes this a pretty successful little score.

VINCENT

Jules, if you give this nimrod fifteen hundred bucks, I'm gonna shoot 'em on general principle.

JULES

You ain't gonna do a goddam thing, now hang back and shut the fuck up. Besides, I ain't givin' it to him. I'm buyin' somethin' for my money. Wanna know what I'm buyin', Ringo?

PUMPKIN

What?

JULES

Your life. I'm giving you that money so I don't hafta kill your ass. You read the Bible?

PUMPKIN

Not regularly.

JULES

There's a passage I got memorized. Ezekiel 25:17. 'The path of the righteous man is beset on all sides by the inequities of the selfish and the tyranny of evil men. Blessed is he who, in the name of charity and good will, shepherds the weak through the valley of the darkness. For he is truly his brother's keeper and the finder of lost children. And I will strike down upon thee with great vengeance and furious anger those who attempt to poison and destroy my brothers. And you will know I am the Lord when I lay my vengeance upon you.' I been sayin' that shit for years. And if you ever heard it, it meant your ass. I never really questioned what it meant. I thought it was just a coldblooded thing to say to a

186

motherfucker 'fore you popped a cap in his ass. But I saw some shit this mornin' made me think twice. Now I'm thinkin', it could mean you're the evil man. And I'm the righteous man. And Mr .45 here he's the shepherd protecting my righteous ass in the valley of darkness. Or it could be you're the righteous man and I'm the shepherd and it's the world that's evil and selfish. I'd like that. But that shit ain't the truth. The truth is you're weak. And I'm the tyranny of evil men. But I'm tryin'. I'm tryin' real hard to be a shepherd.

Jules lowers his gun, lying it on the table.

Pumpkin looks at him, to the money in his hand, then to Yolanda. She looks back.

Grabbing the trash bag full of wallets, the two run out the door.

Jules, who has never risen from his seat the whole time, takes a sip of coffee.

                              (*to himself*)
It's cold.

He pushes it aside.

Vincent appears next to Jules.

                    VINCENT
I think we oughta leave now.

                    JULES
That's probably a good idea.

Vincent throws some money on the table and Jules grabs the briefcase.

Then, to the amazement of the Patrons, the Waitresses, the Cooks, the Busboys, and the Manager, these two bad-ass dudes – wearing UC Santa Cruz and 'I'm with Stupid' T-shirts, swim trunks, thongs and packing .45 Automatics – walk out of the coffee shop together without saying a word.

Miramax Films
presents
A Band Apart
and
Jersey Films production
A film of Quentin Tarantino
PULP FICTION

TIM ROTH	Pumpkin
AMANDA PLUMMER	Honey Bunny
LAURA LOVELACE	Waitress
JOHN TRAVOLTA	Vincent Vega
SAMUEL L. JACKSON	Jules Winnfield
PHIL LAMARR	Marvin
FRANK WHALEY	Brett
BURR STEERS	Roger
BRUCE WILLIS	Butch Coolidge
VING RHAMES	Marsellus Wallace
PAUL CALDERON	Paul
BRONAGH GALLAGHER	Trudi
ROSANNA ARQUETTE	Jody
ERIC STOLZ	Lance
UMA THURMAN	Mia Wallace
JEROME PATRICK HOBAN	Ed Sullivan
MICHAEL GILDEN	Phillip Morris Page
GARY SHORELLE	Ricky Nelson
SUSAN GRIFFITHS	Marilyn Monroe
ERIC CLARK	James Dean
JOSEF PILATO	Dean Martin
BRAD PARKER	Jerry Lewis
STEVE BUSCEMI	Buddy Holly
LORELEI LESLIE	Mamie Van Doren
EMIL SITKA	'Hold Hands You Love Birds'
BRENDA HILLHOUSE	Butch's Mother
CHRISTOPHER WALKEN	Captain Koons
CHANDLER LINDAUER	Young Butch
SY SHER	Klondike
ROBERT RUTH	Sportscaster #1
RICH TURNER	Sportscaster #2
ANGELA JONES	Esmarelda Villalobos

DON BLAKELY	Wilson's Trainer
CARL ALLEN	Dead Floyd Wilson
MARIA DE MEDEIROS	Fabienne
KAREN MARUYAMA	Gawker #1
KATHY GRIFFIN	Herself
VENESSIA VALENTINO	Pedestrian
LINDA KAYE	Shot Lady
DUANE WHITAKER	Maynard
PETER GREENE	Zed
STEPHEN HIBBERT	The Gimp
ALEXIS ARQUETTE	Fourth Man
QUENTIN TARANTINO	Jimmie
VANESSA VALENTINO	Bonnie
HARVEY KEITEL	The Wolf
JULIA SWEENEY	Raquel
ROBERT RUTH	Coffee Shop
LAWRENCE BENDER	Long Hair Yuppie-Scum

Production Manager	PAUL HELLERMAN
Post Production Supervisor	HEIDI VOGEL
1st Assistant Director	FRANCIS R. 'SAM' MAHONY III
2nd Assistant Director	KELLY KIERNAN
2nd-2nd Assistant Director	JOHN 'CRASH' HYDE, JR
Additional 2nd-2nd Assistant Director	WILLIAM PAUL CLARK
Production Accountant	JULIA ZANE
Production Auditor	ANGELIQUE A. COSTANZA
Assistant Accountant	ZANE
Accounting Assistant	ABIGAIL SHEINER
Accounting Intern	CYNTHIA HARDING
Production Coordinator	ANNA-LISA NILSSON
Assistant Production Coordinator	CHERYL CAIN
Production Secretary	BRADLEY MORRIS
Key Office Production Assistant	JAMES 'CHIP' WEIS
Script Supervisor	MARTIN KITROSSER
Location Manager	ROBERT EARL CRAFT
Assistant Location Manager	JOHN A. JOHNSTON
Location Assistant	HALEY B. SWEET
Camera Operator	MICHAEL LEVINE
1st Assistant Cameraman	ZIAD DOUEIRI

2nd Assistant Cameraman	GREGORY C. SMITH
Camera Loader	ANGELO DE LA CRUZ
Steadicam Operator	ROBERT GORLICK
Steadicam 1st Assistant	JOE RITTER
Additional Steadicam Operator	JOHN NULER
Second Unit Photography	ALAN SHERROD
Production Sound Mixer	KEN KING, CAS
Boom Operator	LARRY SCHARF
Key Makeup Artist	MICHELLE BUHLER
Key Hair Supervisor	AUDREE FUTTERMAN
Assistant Makeup and Hair	CHRISTINA BARTOLUCCI
Hair Designer	IAIN JONES
Assistant Hair	LINDA ARNOLD
Wigmaker	BILL FLETCHER
Hair Extensions	DESIGNED BY
	PINY OF BEVERLY HILLS
Assistant Costume Designer	MARY CLAIRE HANNAN
Costumer Supervisor	JACQUELINE ARONSON
Costumers	KRISTIN DANGL
	MARILYN PACHASA
	PATIA PROUTY
Gaffer	VANCE TRUSSELL
Best Boy Electric	ANTHONY HALL
Key Rigging Gaffer	MARC MEISENHEIMER
Electricians	CHRISTOPHER LORING
	ROBERT LEWBEL
	BRUCE JAGODA
	MICHAEL PALMER
Key Grip	MARK SHANE DAVIS
Best Boy grip	ROBERT W. MECKLER
Key Rigging Grip	MICHAEL STOCKS
Dolly Grip	ALAN PARR
Grips	RANDY VERDUGO
	JAMES P. JONES II
	C. ROY NIGRA
	CHRISTOPHER AHERN
	ROBERT STUDENNY
Art Director	CHARLES COLLUM
Set Decorator	SANDY REYNOLDS-WASCO

Lead Man	PETER BORCK
Set designers	DANIEL BRADFORD
	JACEK LISIEWICZ
Construction Coordinator	BRIAN MARKEY
Property Master	JONATHAN HODGES
Assistant Property Master	JOHN FELGATE
Prop Food Stylist	SHOWGRITS, JEAN HODGES
On-Set Dresser	MCPHERSON O. DOWNS
Assistant Decorator	LIZ CHIZ
Buyer	ELLEN BRILL
Art Department Coordinator	EMILY WOLFE
Set Dressers	JOSEPH GRAFMULLER
	DANIEL ROTHENBERG
Swing Gang	STEVEN INGRASSIA
	ED MARTIN II
	MARYANN MATANIC
	SALLY REED
Assistant Art Director	SAMANTHA GORE
Charge Scenic Artist	CHRIS L. WINSLOW
Construction Foreman	RAY MAXWELL
Construction Location Foreman	SHANE HAWKINS
Construction Estimator	CHRIS SCHER

Carpenters

GARY L. BRENNAN	JOSEPH DONTI
TIM GLUECKERT	B. HARRIS
JOSE JIMENEZ	ADAM MARKEY
MICHAEL MCGETTIGAN	DAVE MENDELSON
MARK PETERS	WAYNE SPRINGFIELD

Lead Painter	MARC GILLSON
Painters	GIUSEPPE MAINI III
	AMY SKIUMSBY
	GREG WILSON
Chief Graphic Designer	GERALD MARTINEZ
Graphic Designer	CHRIS CULLEN
Character Artist	RUSSEL VOSSLER
Assembly Editor	JERE P. HUGGINS
1st Assistant Editor	TATIANA S. RIEGEL
Assistant Editor	DONALD LIKOVICH

Second Assistant Editors	KATIE MACK
	RAY NEAPOLITAN
Apprentice Editors	ANDREW DICKLER
	JOHN SOSNOVSKI
Music Editor	ROLF JOHNSON
Video Playback Operator	LARRY MARKART
Unit Publicist	DEBORAH WULIGER
Unit Still Photographer	LINDA R. CHEN
Casting Associate	RUTH LAMBERT
Extras Casting by	RAINBOW CASTING

Stand-Ins

CAMERON	CULLEN CHAMBERS
SCOTT JOHNSTON	RORY K. DAUSON
JEFFREY STEPHAN	GLORIA HYLTON

Stunt Coordinator	KEN LESCO

Stunt Players

CAMERON	CHRIS DOYLE
MARCIA HOLLEY	TERRY JACKSON
MELVIN JONES	LINDA KAYE
HUBIE KERNS JR	SCOTT MCELROY
DENNIS 'DANGER' MADALONE	

Stunt Safety	MATTHEW AVILA
Assistant to the Producer	TONI BAFFO
Assistant to the Producer – Post-Production	COURTNEY MCDONNEL
Assistant to the Director	VICTORIA LUCAI
Coordinator for Miramax	CATHY AGCAYAB RAGONA
Production Legal Services	CARLOS GOODMAN, LICHTER, GROSSMAN & NICHOLS, INC.
Music Legal Services	CODIKOW & CARROLL
Miramax Legal	VICKI CHERKAS
Immigration Legal Services	ROBERT FRAADE, ESQ.
Labor Legal Services	RICHARD W. KOPENHEFER, LOEB AND LOEB
Completion Guarantors	FILM FINANCES, INC.
	KURT WOOLNER
Clearance Supervisor	DONALD ASHER

Post Production Accountant	ANGELIQUE A. COSTANZA
Post Production Coordinator	KARA MAZZOLA
Post Production Assistant	BEN PARKER
Post Production Intern	LIAM CURTIN
Supervising Sound Editor	STEPHEN H. FLICK/MPSE
Supervising ADR Editor	JUDEE FLICK/MPSE

Sound Editors

DAVID BARLETT/MPSE	DEAN BEVILLE
G. W. BROWN	AVRAM DEAN GOLD/MPSE
JOHN HULSMAN	PATRICIO LIBENSON
RICHARD MARX/MPSE	STEWART NELSON
CHARLES E. SMITH/MPSE	SCOTT WEBER

Assistant Sound Editors	JEENA M. PHELPS
	DANA GUSTAFSON
Re-Recording Mixers	RICK ASH
	DEAN A. ZUPANCIC
Pre-Dub Mixer	EZRA DWECK
Dubbing Recordist	LARRY PITMAN
PDL	IVAN JOHNSON
Re-Recorded by	BUENA VISTA SOUND
Foley by	JOAN ROWE
	CATHERINE ROWE
Foley Mixer	EZRA DWECK
ADR Voice Casting	BARBARA HARRIS
ADR Mixer	JEFF COURTIE
Negative Cutter	I.C.E. NEGATIVE CUTTING
Color Timer	MICHAEL STANWICK
Music Consultants	CHUCK KELLEY
	LAURA LOVELACE
Music Coordinator	
For Mind Your Music	MARY RAMOS
Assistants to Music Supervisor	BILLY GOTTLIEB
	KRISTEN BECHT
Music Supervisor for MCA Records	KATHY NELSON

ORIGINAL MOTION PICTURE SOUNDTRACK AVAILABLE ON MCA® CDs AND CASSETTES

'MISIRLOU'
Written by FRED WISE, MILTON LEEDS,
S. K. RUSSELL, NICHOLAS ROUBANIS
Performed by DICK DALE & HIS DEL-TONES
Courtesy of RHINO RECORDS

'STRAWBERRY LETTER #23'
Written by SHUGGIE OTIS
Performed by THE BROTHERS JOHNSON
Courtesy of A & M RECORDS, INC.

'BUSTIN' SURFBOARDS'
Written by GERALD SANDERS, JESSE SANDERS, NORMAN SANDERS
& LEONARD DELANEY
Performed by THE TORNADOES
Courtesy of GNP CRESCENDO RECORDS

'SON OF A PREACHER MAN'
Written by JOHN HURLEY, RONNIE WILKINS
Performed by DUSTY SPRINGFIELD
Courtesy of ATLANTIC RECORDING CORP.
By Arrangement with WARNER SPECIAL PRODUCTS &
POLYGRAM RECORD OPERATIONS LIMITED

'LONESOME TOWN'
Written by BAKER KNIGHT
Performed by RICKY NELSON
Courtesy of EMI RECORDS USA,
A Division of ERG
Under License from CEMA SPECIAL MARKETS

'RUMBLE'
Written by F. L. WRAY, SR., M. COOPER
Performed by LINK WRAY AND HIS RAYMEN

'TEENAGERS IN LOVE'
Written by WILLIAM ROSENAUER
Performed by WOODY THORNE
Courtesy of GNP CRESCENDO RECORDS

'GIRL, YOU'LL BE A WOMAN SOON'
Written by NEIL DIAMOND
Performed by URGE OVERKILL

Courtesy of TOUCH AND GO RECORDS, INC.

'FLOWERS ON THE WALL'
Written by LEWIS DEWITT
Performed by THE STATLER BROTHERS
Courtesy of MERCURY/NASHVILLE
By Arrangement with POLYGRAM SPECIAL MARKETS

'COFFEE SHOP MUSIC'
Courtesy of CAPITOL/OLE GEORG MUSIC

'JUNGLE BOOGIE'
Written by RONALD BELL, CLAYDEN SMITH, GEORGE BROWN,
ROBERT MICKENS, DONALD BOYCE, RICHARD WESTFIELD,
DENNIS THOMAS, ROBERT BELL
Performed by KOOL & THE GANG
Courtesy of POLYGRAM SPECIAL MARKETS

'LET'S STAY TOGETHER'
Written by AL GREEN, AL JACKSON, JR., WILLIE MITCHELL
Performed by AL GREEN
Courtesy of HI RECORDS
Under License from CEMA SPECIAL MARKETS

'BULLWINKLE PART II'
Written by DENNIS ROSE, ERNEST FURROW
Performed by THE CENTURIANS
Courtesy of DEL-FI RECORDS INC.

'WAITIN' IN SCHOOL'
Written by JOHNNY BURNETTE, DORSEY BURNETTE
Performed by GARY SHORELLE
Produced by JOSEPH VITARELLI & NICK VITERELLI

'ACE OF SPADES'
Written by F. L. WRAY, SR., M. COOPER
Performed by LINK WRAY
Courtesy of ROLLERCOASTER RECORDS, ENGLAND

'SINCE I FIRST MET YOU'
Written by H. B. BARNUM
Performed by THE ROBINS
Courtesy of GNP CRESCENDO RECORDS

'YOU NEVER CAN TELL'
Written by CHUCK BERRY

Performed by CHUCK BERRY
Courtesy of MCA RECORDS

'IF LOVE IS A RED DRESS' (HANG ME IN RAGS)
Written by MARIA MCKEE
Performed by MARIA MCKEE
Courtesy of GEFFEN RECORDS

'OUT OF LIMITS'
Written by MICHAEL GORDON
Performed by THE MARKETTS
Courtesy of GO-JO MUSIC

'COMANCHE'
Written by THE REVELS
Performed by THE REVELS
Courtesy of DOWNEY RECORDS

'SURF RIDER'
Written by BOB BOGLE, NOLE EDWARDS, DON WILSON
Performed by THE LIVELY ONES
Courtesy of DEL-FI RECORDS INC.
By Arrangement with RHINO RECORDS

'THE LOSERS' Film Footage Provided by
GORDON FILMS, INC./CASTLE HILL PRODUCTIONS, INC.

'CLUTCH CARGO' Footage Provided by
CORAL PICTURES CORPORATION

'ATTACK OF THE 50 FOOT WOMAN' Poster Courtesy of
WARNER BROS.

'THE YOUNG RACERS' Courtesy of
ORION PICTURES CORPORATION
ALL RIGHTS RESERVED

'THE RING' Magazine Courtesy of LONDON PUBLISHING CO.

Special Thanks to:

SCOTT SPIEGEL	AGNES b.
CHEQUERED FLAG	EMPORIO ARMANI
SLOT CAR RACEWAY	
	ROZANN NEWMAN,
HAMA DESIGN	THE WARNER DRIVE WAREHOUSE
LOU ARKOFF	RINGSIDE PRODUCTS, INC.
CINDY JO STANBERRY	EMANUEL STEWARD

TARANTINO ORDER FORM

As an avid Tarantino fan you will appreciate having his other books delivered direct to your door, and especially appreciate not paying postage and packing. Alternatively you might just like further information about Faber's film list. Either way, please fill in your name and address and return this order form to Faber and Faber.

Please send me the following Tarantino classics:

_____	TRUE ROMANCE	£7.99
_____	RESERVOIR DOGS	£7.99
_____	PULP FICTION	£7.99
_____	NATURAL BORN KILLERS	£7.99
_____	FOUR ROOMS *(Available December 1995)*	£7.99

also available . . .

_____ THE DEFINITIVE PULP FICTION BOX SET
INCLUDES WIDESCREEN VIDEO, SOUNDTRACK CD AND THE
FULL UNCUT SCREENPLAY *(Available November 1995)* £29.99

Total including FREE postage and packing £ _____

TICK HERE FOR YOUR FREE COPY OF THE FABER FILM CATALOGUE _____

I enclose a cheque for £ _____ made payable to Faber and Faber Ltd.

Please charge my ☐ Access ☐ Visa ☐ Amex ☐ Diner's Club ☐ Eurocard

Cardholder _____ Expiry Date _____

Account No. ☐☐☐☐☐☐☐☐☐☐☐☐☐☐☐☐

Name _____

Address _____

Signed _____ Date _____

Send to: Tarantino Promotions, FREEPOST, Faber and Faber Ltd, 3 Queen Square, London WC1N 3BR   FAX 0171 465 0034